PHILOSOPHY IN MINUTES

MARCUS WEEKS

PHILOSOPHY IN MINUTES

MARCUS WEEKS

Quercus

CONTENTS

Introduction

The word "philosophy," like so much else in Western philosophy, is Greek in origin: the original word φιλοσοφια (philosophia) means "love of wisdom," but while that may be a nice description of the subject, it doesn't tell us much about what it actually is.

Perhaps it is best to think of philosophy as being "what philosophers do"—an activity, rather than a study—which is to use the human capacity for rational thought to pose and attempt to answer fundamental questions about the universe and our place in it. This may be a broad definition of a very broad subject, but it is a useful way to distinguish philosophy from other ways in which we try to make sense of the world we live in. At its heart, philosophy is thinking: thinking about why things are the way they are, how best we should live our lives, how we can be certain about what we know, and what meaning, if any, there is to our existence. The same questions are asked by religion and science, but while religion gives answers based on faith or belief, philosophy uses reasoning, and where science provides description, philosophy seeks explanation.

Philosophy as an academic subject studies the ideas of the great thinkers, and it is these that will dominate this book, but it is also something that almost everybody indulges in: we all spend some of our time wondering about the same questions addressed by the great philosophers or discussing them with friends in the bar or over the dinner table. Often, we will disagree, and just as often, we will find no definite answers—philosophers, too, have widely differing opinions, and frequently come up with more questions than answers. But philosophers throughout history have provided us with different ways of looking at these questions, and by understanding their thought processes we can learn how to organize our thoughts and arguments.

Branches of philosophy

The first philosophers that we know of appeared in the sixth century BCE in ancient Greece. As civilizations became well established and more sophisticated, thinkers began to question traditional explanations for the workings of the universe and society, and sought answers based on rational thought rather than convention or religion. The first question they addressed was "What is the world made of?"—the branch of philosophy we now call metaphysics. From this, they also began to question how we can be sure of what we know (the branch of epistemology) and the nature of our existence (ontology). Slowly, they developed a systematic way of analysing their arguments, logic, and techniques of questioning to elicit fundamental ideas. This opened up the field of moral philosophy, or ethics, which is concerned with concepts such as justice, virtue, and happiness, and this in turn led to many philosophers exploring what kind of society we want to live in (giving rise to the branch known as political philosophy).

Raphael's famous fresco *The School of Athens* depicts
key figures in the history of classical philosophy.

Metaphysics

For the first philosophers, the burning question was: "What is everything made of?" At its most basic, this is the central question of a branch of philosophy known as metaphysics. Many of the theories proposed by the ancient Greek philosophers— the notions of elements, atoms, and so on—formed the basis of modern science, which has since provided evidence-based explanations for these fundamental questions.

Metaphysics, however, has evolved into a field of inquiry beyond the realms of science: as well as dealing with the make up of the cosmos, it examines the nature of what exists, including such ideas as the properties of material things, the difference between mind and matter, cause and effect, and the nature of existence, being, and reality (a branch of metaphysics known as ontology). Although some philosophers have challenged the validity of metaphysics in the face of scientific discovery, recent developments in areas such as quantum mechanics have renewed interest in metaphysical theories.

Epistemology

It soon became apparent to philosophers in ancient Greece that there was an underlying problem with all the questions they were attempting to answer, best summed up by the simple question: "How can we know that?" This, and similar questions about what sort of thing we can know (if anything), how we can acquire knowledge, and the nature of knowledge itself, have preoccupied Western philosophy ever since, forming the branch of philosophy known as epistemology.

Some philosophers believe that we acquire knowledge by experience and through the evidence provided to us by our senses—a view known as empiricism; others think that knowledge is primarily acquired by a process of reasoning, a view known as rationalism. The division between empiricism and rationalism helped to define various schools of philosophy until the 19th century. Other areas of epistemology, meanwhile, deal with the connection between knowledge and concepts such as truth and belief.

Ontology

Considered to be the major branch of metaphysics, ontology is the field of philosophy that examines the nature of existence and reality. It is distinct from epistemology in that it is not concerned with our knowledge of a thing, but addresses the questions of whether something actually exists, and what sort of things can be said to exist.

As well as trying to establish what can be said to exist, ontology also attempts to identify the properties of the things that exist, and categorize them according to these properties and the relationships between them. Naturally, this entails an examination of the meaning of the terms "existence," "being," and "reality"—a central concern of ontology—and concepts such as the substance or essence of an object, its identity, and the difference between concrete and abstract objects: can concepts such as "love" and "memory" be said to exist in the same way as a table or a rock?

Logic

In seeking answers to questions about the universe and our place in it, philosophy is distinguished from religion or mere convention by its use of reasoning. A philosopher proposes ideas as a result of thought, and has to justify his or her assertions with rational argument. Various techniques have been devised to show whether an argument is valid or fallacious, forming the branch of philosophy known as logic.

In simple terms, logic is the process of inferring a conclusion from statements known as premises, either deriving a general principle from specific examples (inductive reasoning) or reaching a conclusion from general statements (deductive reasoning). The classical form of logical argument, the syllogism, consisting of two premises and a conclusion, was formalized by Aristotle (see page 84) and remained the mainstay of philosophical logic until advances in mathematical logic brought in new ideas in the 19th century, and symbolic logic opened up new fields of philosophy in the 20th century.

All men are
mortal

Socrates is
a man

Therefore
Socrates is
mortal

Moral philosophy and ethics

While the earliest philosophers sought to understand the wider universe, it was not long before philosophy turned its attention to humans themselves, and the way we lead our lives. The idea of virtue was central to life in classical society, but difficult to define; concepts of good and evil, happiness, courage, and morality became the subjects of debate in the branch of philosophy known as ethics, or moral philosophy.

In trying to ascertain the nature of a virtuous life, philosophers raised the question of what the goal of life should be—what is its "purpose"? How should we lead our lives, and to what end? The concept of the "good life," *eudaimonia*, figured largely in Greek philosophy, and embodies not only a virtuous life, but also a happy one. Several different schools of thought emerged as to how this "good life" could be achieved, including the cynics, who believed in harmony with nature, the Epicureans, who believed pleasure to be the greatest good, and the stoics, who believed in acceptance of things beyond our control.

Political philosophy

Where ethics and moral philosophy seek to define virtue and what constitutes the "good life," the closely related branch of political philosophy examines the nature of concepts such as justice, and what sort of society can best allow its citizens to lead "good" lives. The problems of how society should be organized and governed were of paramount importance not only to classical Greece, but also in the development of nation-states in China at much the same time, and elsewhere as new civilizations emerged.

As a branch of philosophy, political philosophy deals with ideas of justice, liberty, and rights, and the relationship between a state and its citizens. It also examines various forms of government, such as monarchy, aristocracy, oligarchy, tyranny, and democracy, how each affects the rights and freedoms of the individual, and how they exert their authority through rule of law.

Aesthetics

As the classical Greek philosophers sought to define concepts such as virtue and justice, giving rise to the branches of moral and political philosophy, they also asked the question: "What is beauty?" This is the fundamental question of aesthetics. As a branch of philosophy, aesthetics tries to establish what, if any, objective criteria there are for judging whether something is beautiful, but in a wider sense also examines all aspects of art—including the very basic question "What is art?"

At various times in history, the emphasis of aesthetics has moved from what constitutes art to the religious or sociopolitical significance of works of art, a general theory of our appreciation of art and how we perceive it, and the process of artistic creativity itself. Philosophical and ethical problems are also raised when considering such matters as the authenticity of a work of art or the sincerity of its creator.

Eastern and Western philosophies

Although the tradition that began in ancient Greece still tends to dominate philosophical discussion in the Western world, philosophy is by no means restricted to that single tradition. Thinkers such as Laozi and Confucius in China also founded their own traditions of philosophy from different starting points, as, arguably, did Buddha in India. For them, and subsequent Eastern philosophers, questions of metaphysics were considered to be adequately explained by religion—hence the Eastern traditions are much more focused on concepts of virtue and the way in which we should lead our lives. In China especially, this moral philosophy was adopted by the ruling dynasties and took on a political dimension. Eastern and Western philosophies developed very separately until the 19th century, when European philosophers, notably Schopenhauer, began to take an interest in Indian religious and philosophical thought (see page 272). Elements of Eastern philosophy have subsequently been incorporated into some branches of Western philosophy.

In India and China,
the differences
between philosophy
and religion are less
clear than in
the West.

Philosophy vs. religion

Religion and philosophy offer two distinctly different approaches to answering our questions about the world about us—religion through belief, faith, and divine revelation, and philosophy through reason and argument—but they often cover much the same ground and are sometimes interrelated. Eastern philosophy developed side by side with religion, and Islam saw no incompatibility between its theology and the philosophy it inherited from the classical world, but the relationship between Western philosophy and Christianity was very often uneasy. Church authorities in the medieval period saw philosophy as a challenge to their dogma, and Christian philosophers risked being branded as heretics for attempting to incorporate Greek philosophical ideas into Christian doctrine. But more than that, philosophy also brought into question issues of belief as opposed to knowledge, faith as opposed to reason—questioning, for example, whether there was any evidence for miracles or even whether the existence of God could be proved.

Philosophy and science

Throughout much of the history of philosophy, there was no such thing as science in its modern form: in fact, it was from philosophical inquiry that modern science has evolved. The questions that metaphysics set out to answer about the structure and substance of the universe prompted theories that later became the foundations of "natural philosophy," the precursor of what we now call physics. The process of rational argument, meanwhile, underpins the "scientific method."

Since the 18th century, many of the original questions of metaphysics have been answered by observation, experiment, and measurement, and philosophy appeared to be redundant in these areas. Philosophers have since changed their focus to examine science itself. Some, like Hume, challenged the validity of inductive reasoning in science (see page 226), while others sought to clarify the meaning of terms used by science, opening up a "philosophy of science" that considers areas such as scientific ethics and the way science makes progress.

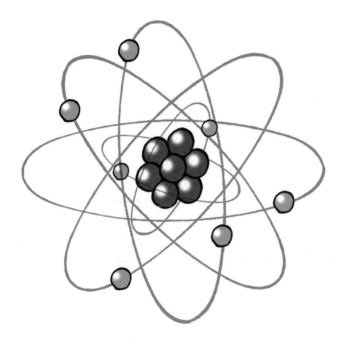

Greek philosophy

The beginnings of Western philosophy are closely linked to the rapid growth of Greek culture and society from around the sixth century BCE. In addition to mainland Greece and the Greek islands, Greeks had settled throughout the eastern Mediterranean, and southern Italy and Sicily. It was in one of these colonies, Miletus on the coast of modern Turkey, that the first known philosophers appeared. Led by Thales, the Milesian school of philosophy inspired subsequent generations, and the practice of philosophical thought and discussion rapidly spread across the Greek world. Athens proved to be the ideal place for philosophy to flourish, and produced perhaps the three most influential philosophers of all time—Socrates, Plato, and Aristotle. They were followed by four main schools of thought: the cynics, skeptics, Epicureans, and stoics. Greek influence reached its height under Alexander the Great, but after his death in 323 BCE, Greece fragmented into conflicting factions and its cultural influence also waned, to be overtaken by the increasingly powerful Roman Empire.

Thales of Miletus

Sometime around the beginning of the sixth century BCE in the Greek colony of Miletus, a man called Thales, dissatisfied with traditional explanations for the workings of the universe, sought to find his own answers by rational thought. As far as we know, he was the first to do this, and is considered to be the first philosopher. The problem that most concerned him, and became the abiding interest for all of the "pre-Socratic" philosophers, was "What is the world made of?"

Thales's answer was a surprising one: he believed everything was made from a single element: water. His reasoning was that water is essential to all life and appears in several forms— as well as a liquid, it is solid when cold, and a gas when hot. What's more, the solid earth seemed to be floating on water, so it probably emerged from water and was therefore made of water, as was everything in the universe. Thales idea was perhaps not as simplistic as it first seems, now modern science shows us that all matter can ultimately be reduced to energy.

Thales' cosmology took inspiration from the fact that much of Earth's surface is indeed covered by water.

Anaximander
and Anaximenes

One of the features of philosophy that distinguishes it from other ways of looking at the world is that its students are encouraged not to accept the conclusions of their teachers, but to discuss, argue, and even disagree. This is exactly what happened in the very first school of philosophy, the Milesian school founded by Thales: his student Anaximander asked if the Earth was supported by water (as Thales argued—see page 32), then what supported that? He suggested that the Earth was a drum-shaped cylinder hanging in space, with one of the flat surfaces forming the world we live on. Anaximander also had a pupil, Anaximenes, who said that the world was self-evidently flat and floated on air. Using the same sort of arguments as Thales, he concluded that the single element from which everything is made is air. Although the conclusions of the Milesian philosophers seem to us hopelessly wrong in the light of later scientific discoveries, the process of reasoning used to reach them—especially argument and counterargument— still forms the basis for philosophical investigation.

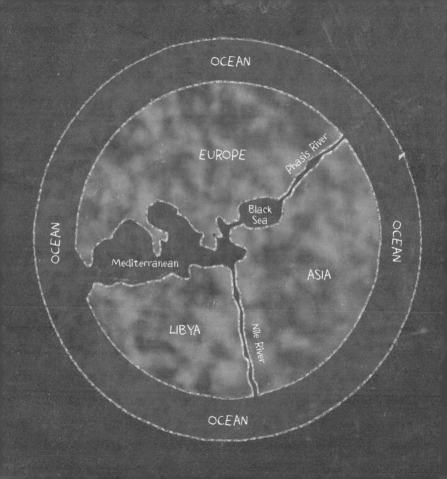

Infinite regress

The argument Anaximander used to challenge his teacher's theory of the Earth floating on water involved an idea that crops up in several strands of philosophy. If the world is supported by a body of water, then what supports the water? And then, what supports *that*? And so on, *ad infinitum*. The same pattern can be seen in arguments involving cause and effect: if something causes something else, then what caused *that*? This apparently unending chain is called an infinite regress. Some philosophers saw the existence of infinite regress as proof that the universe is eternal, but many were uncomfortable with the idea and proposed that there must be an original or first cause for everything (an idea that chimes with the modern theory of the Big Bang). For some, the first cause or "prime mover" was an abstract idea akin to pure thought or reason, but, for medieval Christian philosophers especially, it was God: indeed, the idea of a first cause was at the heart of Thomas Aquinas's cosmological argument for the existence of God (see page 140).

e idea of a screen within a screen within a screen, like an infinite series
reflections, embodies the troublesome concept of infinite regress.

Heraclitus:
everything is in flux

In contrast to the school of philosophy founded by Thales at Miletus, just along the Ionian coast in the city of Ephesus lived a solitary thinker, Heraclitus, with very different philosophical views. Rather than suggesting a single element from which everything was derived, he suggested an underlying principle—that of change. Heraclitus saw everything as consisting of opposing properties or tendencies, which come together to make up the substance of the world. The analogy he gave was that the path up a mountain is the same as the path down.

In this theory, known as the "unity of opposites," the tension and contradiction of opposing forces is what creates reality, but it is inherently unstable. Therefore, everything is constantly changing: everything is in flux. Just as the water in a river is constantly flowing onward, but the river itself remains the same, that which we consider to be permanent, unchanging reality consists not of objects, but processes.

Pythagoras: a universe ruled by numbers

Pythagoras was born on the island of Samos off the Ionian coast, but unlike the other Ionian philosophers he apparently did not stay there for long. He is believed to have traveled around the Mediterranean, until, aged about 40, he set up a pseudoreligious sect in the Greek colony of Croton in southern Italy. This eccentric genius had a particular talent for mathematics, making connections between geometry and arithmetic through the idea of squared and cubed numbers, and recognizing mathematical ratios inherent in music and acoustics. He also brought this knowledge to bear on philosophical questions, arguing that there was a structure to the cosmos (a word he coined) based on mathematical laws. The positions and movements of the heavenly bodies, he suggested, were analogous to the ratios of musical harmony (the so-called "harmony of the spheres"). Pythagoras was the first to connect mathematics and philosophy, and the founder of a distinguished line of philosophers, including Descartes, Leibniz, and Russell, who were also great mathematicians.

Pythagoras is often credited with discovering the mathematical equations relating to musical harmonies, supposedly after hearing the different notes emitted when hammers of different weights struck an anvil.

Xenophanes—
evidence and true belief

Like Pythagoras, Xenophanes of Colophon was an Ionian-born philosopher who traveled widely, spending most of a reputedly long life moving from one Greek colony to another. His theory of cosmic composition involved two alternating extremes of wet and dry—neatly combining the Milesian ideas of pure elements of air and water (see pages 32 and 34) with Heraclitus's theory of opposites (see page 42). What what was more significant, however, was the fact that he used fossils to back up his idea that the world was once covered by water—one of the first examples of evidence-based argument.

Xenophanes is also credited with being the first philosopher to deal with questions of epistemology, suggesting that when we say we "know" something, that knowledge is actually only a "true belief"—a hypothesis good enough for us to work from. A "truth of reality" does exist, but this will always be beyond our human understanding; the best we can do is refine our hypotheses to continually get nearer to it.

Parmenides: monism

Around the beginning of the fifth century BCE, the center of philosophy moved from Ionia to southern Italy, and in particular to the Greek colony of Elea. The founder of what became the "Eleatic school" was Parmenides, who produced a counterargument to Heraclitus's idea that everything is in flux (see page 38). Parmenides's argument was based on the idea that that you can't say of "nothing" that it exists, and therefore there can never have been nothing: it cannot be true that everything came from nothing, so everything must always have existed—and will always exist since it can't *become* nothing either. The universe, then, is completely full of *something*, which Parmenides believed was a single entity: all is one, uniform, unchanging, and eternal. This view is known as monism.

However, Parmenides was also at pains to point out that there is also a world of appearances—the illusory world in which we live. This distinction between reality and perception was to become an important idea in later Western philosophy.

Zeno's paradoxes

Like his mentor Parmenides, Zeno of Elea (not to be confused with Zeno of Citium, see page 104) believed that "all is one" and that change is impossible. To support his arguments, he used paradoxes—examples that seem to be logically sound but reach a conclusion that flies in the face of common sense. For example, Zeno pointed out that, at any instant in time, an arrow in flight is in one particular place and therefore not moving; and since time is made up of successive instants in which the arrow is motionless, the arrow cannot be moving.

A different problem of motion is tackled in the paradox of Achilles and the tortoise: in a race together, Achilles gives the tortoise a head start, and they both start running at their different speeds. When Achilles reaches the point where the tortoise started, the tortoise has advanced a shorter distance ahead; by the time Achilles has caught up to this point, the tortoise has moved further on, and so on—so Achilles can never catch up with the tortoise, let alone overtake him.

According to Zeno, the tortoise will always beat Achilles if it is given a head start.

Sorites paradox

Many philosophers have found paradoxes useful, helping to clarify ideas by taking them to a logical, if absurd, conclusion. One of the best known is the "liar paradox" associated with Epimenides of Crete who asserted that "Cretans are always liars." While some paradoxes can be shown to use invalid logical reasoning, others point to failings of logic itself. One example is the "sorites paradox" (from the Greek *soros*, a heap). One grain of sand is obviously not a heap, and nor are two grains of sand, or even three … and if we continue this progression then 10,000 grains don't make a heap either!

The problem here is with our system of logic, where things are either true or false; it's either a heap or not a heap, and there's nothing in between. Another version of this paradox is that of the balding man—but here we can at least recognize various degrees of thinning. The shortcomings of "bivalent" logic can also be seen in other areas of philosophy, such as ethics, where it may be too simple to think in terms of right and wrong.

The four elements

The question of what the universe is made of was still a major concern of Greek philosophers in the fifth century BCE. Empedocles, a native of Akragas in Sicily, continued the Milesian line of thought that everything was composed of a single element (see page 32). But he took this a step further, identifying four distinct elements—earth, water, air, and fire—which in different proportions formed all the different substances in the universe. Developing his ideas from the monism of Parmenides (see page 44), he argued that these elements must therefore be eternal and unalterable, but reasoned that change was possible if some sort of force altered the mixture of elements. He suggested that two opposing physical forces, which he poetically called "Love" and "Strife," caused attraction or separation of the elements and brought about changes in the composition of substances. His classification of the substances later known as the four classical elements was widely accepted by philosophers, and was a cornerstone of alchemy until the Renaissance.

Empedocles's notion of the four elements—earth, water, fire, and air—persisted into medieval times and influenced the growth of alchemy, along with ideas such as the trinity of body, mind, and soul, as represented in this woodcut.

Democritus and Leucippus: atomism

A theory of matter proposed by Leucippus and his pupil Democritus was less influential at the time than the "four elements" proposed by their contemporary Empedocles (see page 50), but in retrospect seems closer to modern scientific understanding. They suggested that everything in the universe is composed of minute, unalterable, and indivisible particles, which they called atoms (from the Greek *atomos*, uncuttable). These, they argued, are free to move through empty space, combining in constantly changing configurations.

The assertion there is such a thing as a void, an empty space, may be one reason these ideas were originally considered unacceptable. According to their theory, the number of atoms is infinite, and different kinds of atoms with different characteristics determine the properties of the substance they form together. Because the atoms are indestructible, when a substance, or even a human body, decays, its atoms are dispersed and reconstituted in another form.

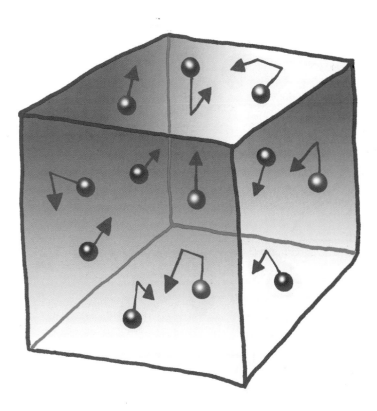

Athenian philosophy

In the fifth century BCE, Athens emerged as the major *polis*, or city-state, of mainland Greece. Already a significant military and trading power in the region, social and political reforms initiated by the statesman Solon led to Athens adopting a form of democracy in 508 BCE. The ensuing prosperity and security allowed a flourishing of culture in the city—especially in the arts of music, theater, and poetry—and attracted intellectuals from other parts of the Greek world. Among them were Anaxagoras, from Ionia, and Protagoras, from Abdera in Thrace, who introduced the idea of philosophy to the city.

Athens was ideally suited to fostering philosophy and quickly became the center of Greek philosophy, producing some of the most influential thinkers of all time. But more than that, Athenian cultural and political life influenced a change in the direction of philosophy, shifting emphasis from metaphysical concerns to the more humanist questions of moral and political philosophy.

The sophists
and relativism

A longside the new democracy in Athens came a new legal system, and with it a class of advocates who, for a fee, would argue cases for clients or teach them how to use rhetoric and rational argument. Out of this class emerged a school of philosophers known as sophists, led by Protagoras, who used similar techniques to examine ideas of morality. Central to sophism is the idea (very much a lawyer's stance), that there is more than one side to every argument, and we must take into account the perspective of the people involved.

For instance, the weather in Athens is clement to an Athenian, but seems hot to a visitor from Greenland, and cold to one from Egypt. This idea that there is no absolute truth and that there is only relative, subjective value, is known as relativism, and was summed up by Protagoras as "man is the measure of all things." Although this stance seems a reasonable one, the relativist approach does pose problems for moral philosophy: are there *really* no moral absolutes?

Socrates and
the dialectical method

The great philosopher Socrates was one of the foremost critics of sophism: he not only condemned their charging for wisdom, but also felt that philosophical inquiry should aim to elicit truth, not simply win a debate. However, this did not stop him adopting some of the sophists' techniques of argument; having studied earlier philosophers, he realized that their method of reasoning was weak and based on speculation.

Socrates set out to rigorously examine fundamental questions through reasoned argument in dialogue with others of opposing views—a technique now known as the dialectical method. His approach was to start from the idea that "I only know that I know nothing," and through discussion with a person or group try to arrive at agreed definitions. Starting with a seemingly simple question such as "What is justice?" he would interrogate his subject relentlessly with further questions that exposed inconsistencies and contradictions, challenging assumptions and conventional beliefs in order to provide insights.

Socrates and the origins of moral philosophy

It was not only in his methods that Socrates differed from most pre-Socratic philosophers; as an active participant in Athenian politics, he also felt that their metaphysical speculations were largely irrelevant to human life. And despite his alleged contempt for the sophists (see page 56), Socrates was as influenced by their concentration on human concerns as he was by their methods. What interested him were concepts such as justice, virtue, courage, and, above all, truth—abstract ideas prompted by the structure of Athenian society, and what we now recognize as the concerns of moral philosophy.

In his philosophical discussions with the citizens of Athens, Socrates sought definitions for these concepts, trying to narrow down their properties by dialectical discourse and reasoning. He professed no knowledge or opinions, but his line of questioning often implied some underlying ideas of right and wrong and led the discussion to conclusions that he believed would help people to behave more morally and live a "good life."

Statues of the classical virtues at the Musée d'Orsay, Paris.

The life unexamined

Socrates wrote nothing, founded no school, and had only a small group of followers, mainly young students. Yet he was well known in Athens for simply walking around the city engaging people in discussion, and was to become regarded as one of the greatest of all philosophers. Not everyone appreciated his ideas at the time, however: popular dramatists lampooned him as a figure of fun, while the establishment viewed him with suspicion for challenging conventional opinions. He was for a time dismissed as a sophist—a mere professional debater—but eventually he was accused of corrupting the morals of young people and not believing in the city gods. Tried and found guilty, he was offered the chance to renounce his philosophical inquiries to avoid the death sentence, but chose instead to drink the hemlock offered to him, saying that the life unexamined is not worth living. One of his followers, the young Plato, wrote a moving account of his trial and death in the *Apologia*, and through his other writings preserved Socrates's ideas for posterity.

Eudaimonia—
the good life

At the heart of Socrates's constant questioning was the question of how best we should live our lives. By trying to narrow down exactly what we mean by terms such as justice, virtue, honor, and courage, he believed people could learn to behave in a way that was more just, virtuous, honorable, or courageous, and live a good life. Of course, this in turn raised the question of what exactly we mean by living a "good life," which the Greek philosophers called *eudaimonia*.

The search for a definition of *eudaimonia* and its attributes became a central concern of Greek moral philosophy. It seemed obvious that a "good" life should be a happy one, but by happiness do we mean contentment, or sensual pleasure? And what sort of lifestyle would bring about most happiness? For Socrates, the good life was about more than pleasure and happiness, and included the very ideals he examined in such detail: justice, honor, courage, and so on—all considered to be constituent parts of virtue, in its widest sense.

Virtue and knowledge

As well as being professional advocates and orators, the sophists (see page 56) used their debating skills as educators. They not only trained their clients in rhetoric and argument, but also in ethics, in courses similar to those offered today by lifestyle coaches (and to a similar clientele of the rich and ambitious). What they taught was *arete*, which can be translated as "excellence," but carries a notion of reaching one's full potential. The notion of *arete* played a central role in the concept of the "good life," and was effectively synonymous with the Greek idea of "virtue." Socrates believed that to live a life of virtue, you have to know what *arete* is, and so reached the conclusion that virtue *is* knowledge. He argued that virtue is necessary *and* sufficient for the good life. Someone who does not know virtue cannot lead a good and happy life, and someone who knows virtue cannot lead anything other than a good and happy life. He summed this up in the apparently paradoxical statement "no one desires evil"—because virtue is knowledge, one can only do wrong out of ignorance.

A statue of Arete, goddess of virtue, amid the ruins of the library at Ephesus, Turkey.

Beginnings of political philosophy

Perhaps because Athens had established a form of democracy that demanded the active participation of its citizens (or at least, a certain class of its citizens), Athenian philosophers soon began to apply the ideas of moral philosophy to society as a whole. Concepts of virtue, such as justice and freedom, were seen to relate not only to the individual, but also to the *polis*, the city-state.

This new field of ethics thus became known as politics— "things to do with the *polis*"—or political philosophy. Like the broader study of moral philosophy, its main concern for Greek philosophers was in defining the virtues appropriate to the state, but also included the idea of *eudaimonia*: how should an entire society be organized to best allow its citizens to live a "good life"? By extension, this involved an examination of the various ways in which a state could be governed, the means by which its laws could be made and enforced, and the relationship between the individual and the state.

The Pnyx, a hill in Athens where in the sixth century BCE Athenians held the popular assemblies that evolved into the world's first democratic system.

Plato and the
Socratic dialogues

Since Socrates wrote nothing himself, almost everything we know about his philosophy comes from the works of his protégé Plato. Fortunately, nearly all of Plato's prolific writings have survived, and Socrates figures largely in many of them. As well as accounts of Socrates's ideas, such as the description of his trial in the *Apologia* (see page 62), Plato embraced his mentor's idea of the dialectic and presented a large number of his philosophical works in the form of dialogues. In most of these, Socrates appears as the principal character, quizzing other philosophers and public figures.

These "Socratic dialogues" present us with a problem, however: Plato is effectively putting words into the mouths of his characters—so how much of the philosophy underlying them is Socrates, and how much Plato? Fortunately, Plato left us enough work that is clearly his own to get a good idea of his original ideas, but Socrates's influence on him was enormous, and it is not always easy to distinguish the two.

Statues of Socrates (left)
and Plato at the Academy
of Arts in Athens.

Plato's theory of Forms

Socrates's method of using dialectical questioning to establish the fundamental essence of a concept set Plato in the direction of one of his most important ideas, the theory of Forms or Ideas (given capital letters here to distinguish these from other meanings of the words). He, too, sought to find definitions, and find out what it is that makes a thing exactly the sort of thing that it is. When we see a bed, for example, we recognize it as a bed even though it may differ in many ways from all the beds we have ever seen. We have, Plato, argued, an idea of an ideal Form of *bed* in our minds. Similarly, we can recognize a circle, no matter how badly drawn, because we have in mind the Idea, or Form, of a perfect circle, even though such a thing cannot exist. There are also Forms for abstract concepts as well as concrete objects. These ideal Forms exist in a world separate from our earthly existence, but we have an innate knowledge of them that can be accessed by rational thought—in contrast to the imperfect perceptions available through our senses.

The regular geometrical shapes known as the Platonic solids were seen as some of the most perfect of all Forms.

Tetrahedron

Cube

Octahedron

Dodecahedron

Icosahedron

Plato's cave

To illustrate his theory of Forms (see page 72), Plato asked his students to imagine a cave, deep enough underground that no daylight reaches it, holding prisoners who have been chained all their lives so that all they can see is its back wall. Behind them is another wall, and beyond this a fire. People along the top of this wall, in front of the first, carry objects on their heads so that the shadows of these things are cast on the wall in front of the prisoners.

As this is all they ever see, Plato argued, the prisoners would assume that these shadows are the only reality, but if they could free themselves, they would discover they were mere shadows of reality. They would also find the light dazzling at first, and if they could make their way to the world outside the cave, would be temporarily blinded by the sunlight. If they returned to the cave, however, they would be unable to see because of the darkness. So it is with the illusory nature of our perception of the world compared to the world of Forms.

Morality and religion

Philosophy developed from the human desire to find rational explanations for things without recourse to religion. The increasing sophistication of Greek society led to a feeling that, despite a still-widespread belief in the gods and their influence in the world, they had become more remote from human life. Most philosophers saw religion as irrelevant to their thinking, but with the emergence of moral philosophy the question of divine influence resurfaced.

Plato tackled this problem in his dialogue *Eurthyphro*, posing the question: "Is the pious loved by the gods because it is pious, or is it pious because they love it?" In other words, is our morality determined by religion, or do we devise it ourselves and incorporate it into our religion? Plato took this further, suggesting that we have some innate concept (in his terms, a knowledge of the Forms) of good and evil. This question of how far morality is human or God-given became a particular preoccupation for medieval Christian and Islamic philosophers.

Plato vs. Aristotle

In the early fourth century BCE, Plato founded a school of philosophy known as the Academy. Among his pupils was Aristotle, who had moved to Athens from Macedonia to study with him. Aristotle turned out to be as brilliant a thinker as Plato himself, but the two could hardly have been more different. While Plato thought in broad terms about abstract concepts, Aristotle was meticulous and practical; Plato's ideas were based on a world of Ideas, Aristotle's more down to earth.

As is almost invariably true of philosophers, their personalities are apparent in their approaches to philosophy. Plato and Aristotle held almost diametrically opposed views of how we understand and acquire knowledge of the world, which remained a basic division of schools of thought in epistemology until the 19th century. Despite their disagreements, they had a mutual respect for one another, and Aristotle remained at Plato's Academy for about 20 years, only founding his own rival school, the Lyceum, several years after Plato's death.

Aristotle (right) and Plato, as depicted in Raphael's fresco *The School of Athens*.

Scientific observation and classification

Aristotle was both a keen naturalist and an almost obsessive organizer. After Plato's death, he spent several years in Asia Minor studying the plants and animals. He identified characteristics, similarities, and differences, and eventually produced a systematic classification of living things. Presented as a hierarchy from simple plants and animals to humans, it was later known as the *scala naturae* or the "great chain of being."

Aristotle also took an interest in the physical sciences, or "natural philosophy," and advocated the same methodical approach: observation, organization, and a rational process of deriving conclusions. This was a radical departure from the pure reasoning advocated by previous philosophers and a major step toward a scientific method of examining the world. He applied the same approach to his philosophy as a whole, organizing and classifying his work in branches, but at the same time pointing out connections and building probably the first comprehensive system of philosophy.

Aristotle: knowledge from experience

From his study of the natural world, Aristotle derived a theory of how we acquire knowledge that was diametrically opposed to that of Plato. He realized that what he knew about plants and animals had come through his observations and concluded that *all knowledge* came from experience.

For example, when he saw a dog, he could recognize it as a dog, even though dogs come in all shapes and sizes. Plato explained this as coming from an innate knowledge of a world of Forms (see page 72). But Aristotle reasoned that it was because he had seen a number of dogs before and gradually built an idea of what constitutes a dog from their common characteristics—from the various separate instances of "dog," he had derived a concept of "dogginess." In a similar way, we understand abstract concepts such as justice or virtue from our experience of various instances of them. Knowledge of anything is therefore empirical—it is only after experience of something via our senses that we can apply the process of rational thought.

Logic and the syllogism

Like all philosophers, Aristotle sought to justify his theories with rational arguments. But he was not content with the simple reasoning used by the early philosophers, nor even the dialectical method developed by Socrates. Instead, he proposed a system of logic whereby the information in two statements or "premises" can be used to reach a conclusion. For example, from the premises "All men are mortal" and "Socrates is a man," we can infer the conclusion "Socrates is mortal."

In the first formal study of logic, Aristotle broke down this form of logical argument, known as a syllogism, into three parts: a major premise, a minor premise, and a conclusion. Each of these parts contains two terms, presented in various forms such as "All A are B," "Some A are B," "No A are B," or "Some A are not B." Using his talent for analysis and classification, he then categorized the possible combinations of the different forms of premise and conclusion, identifying those that presented valid arguments, and those that were invalid.

"All A are B"   "No A are B"

Universal   Contraries   Universal
affirmatives   negatives

Subalterns   Contradictories   Subalterns

Particular   Particular
affirmatives   Subcontraries   negatives

"Some A are B"   "Some A are not B"

The square of opposition is a way of representing relationships between the
four different types of proposition used in syllogisms.

The four causes and the nature of being

Because of his practical disposition and interest in natural and physical sciences, Aristotle did not restrict himself to moral philosophy as much as Socrates and Plato had done. As well as examining the way in which we acquire knowledge of the world around us, he questioned what made things the way they are—the nature of being. He believed that we cannot have any knowledge of something until we understand its "why": how it came to be, and in particular the explanation for change or movement of an object or event. Aristotle suggested four distinct categories of explanation, which he called "causes," of how a thing has come about:

- material cause (the material the thing is composed of).
- formal cause (the structure of the thing, or its blueprint).
- efficient cause (more akin to our modern understanding of cause, meaning the outside agency or event that brings it about).
- final cause (what a thing has come about for—its purpose or aim, but in a very wide sense).

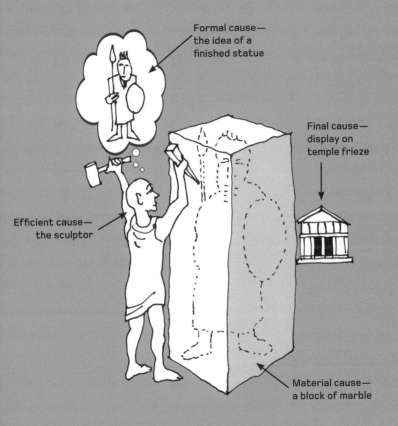

Formal cause—
the idea of a
finished statue

Final cause—
display on
temple frieze

Efficient cause—
the sculptor

Material cause—
a block of marble

Republic and *Politics*

Both Plato and Aristotle extended their theories into political philosophy, examining how best society could be organized. Unsurprisingly, each took a different approach and reached a different conclusion. Plato's *Republic* described his vision of a somewhat authoritarian city-state governed by specially educated philosopher-kings, whose knowledge of the Forms of virtue made them uniquely qualified to rule.

Aristotle applied a more systematic approach in his *Politics*. He analysed the possible forms of government, categorizing them by criteria of "Who rules?" (a single person, a select few, or the people?) and "On whose behalf?" (themselves, or the state?). He identified three forms of true constitution: monarchy, aristocracy, and polity (or constitutional government). These all ruled for the common good, but when perverted, became tyranny, oligarchy, and democracy. Given a choice, Aristotle believed that polity was the optimal form of government, with democracy the least harmful of the perverted forms.

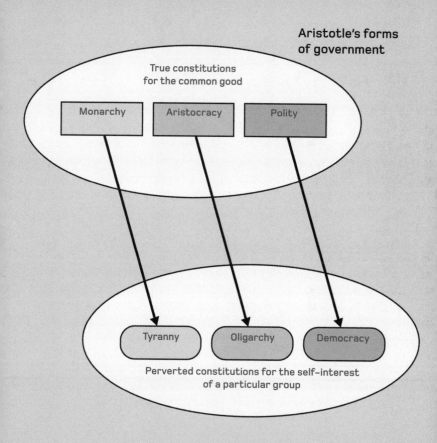

Ethics and the Golden Mean

Socrates was largely concerned with refining definitions of such things as virtues, in an attempt to discover their essential quality—a quest that continued in the moral philosophy of Plato and Aristotle. But although they apparently sought an absolute definition, they were wary of focusing it too narrowly, preferring to think of a sort of scale of degrees of each virtue. The idea of moderation figured largely in Greek thought from earliest times, encapsulated in the maxim "nothing in excess," and exemplified in the ancient myth of Icarus.

Moderation was an especially important element of Aristotle's ethics. He envisaged the spectrum of a virtue not as ranging from extremes of "good" to "bad," but with an optimal value in the middle of the scale—the so-called Golden Mean. For example, courage is considered a virtue, but when taken to one extreme becomes recklessness and at the other extreme cowardice, both of which are undesirable traits; similarly, justice can be seen to have extremes of severity and leniency.

Ignoring advice to take a middle course between sea and sky, Icarus was tempted to fly too high; the heat of the sun melted the wax of his wings and he fell to his death.

Beauty

It was not only virtues that Socrates and his followers sought to define. One of his seemingly simple questions was: "What is beauty?"—the starting point for the field of aesthetics (see page 22). As with virtue, it is easier to recognize individual instances of beautiful things than to pin down beauty itself.

For the classical Greeks, however, certain common characteristics could be identified, especially proportion, symmetry, balance, and harmony. These reflected both an interest in mathematics that had its origins in Pythagoras's analysis of musical harmony and proportion, and the idea of the Golden Mean of Aristotle's ethics (see page 90). But in seeking a definition for beauty, other questions arose: are these criteria universal, or is beauty in the eye of the beholder and simply a matter of taste? Is something beautiful because we find it beautiful, or is there something inherent that makes it beautiful? And is there a difference between the beauty we see in nature and the manmade beauty of a work of art?

Judging a work of art

Greek culture flourished in the classical period. In the time of the great Athenian philosophers, it produced great works of poetry, theater, music, architecture, and art. Not everyone recognized their excellence, however—Plato, for example, distrusted all the arts as distracting and poor imitations of the ideal Forms of beauty and goodness. But how then *should* we judge a work of art? If we simply regard it as a matter of taste, we run the risk of confusing our emotional response with an objective appraisal, the so-called "affective fallacy." It may be just as misleading to seek meaning in art: we may try to discover the artist's intention, but find this at odds with our appraisal of his or her work. In the case of Wagner, for example, do his repugnant racism and personal arrogance detract from the worth of his music, or is this an instance of the "intentional fallacy"? Modern art often falls outside of our narrow definitions, and forgeries and reproductions challenge our perceptions of the role of the artist, raising the perennial question, "What is art?"

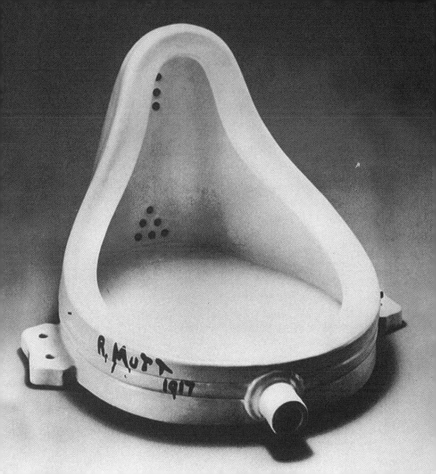

Cynics: Diogenes

The trio of Socrates, Plato, and Aristotle proved something of a hard act to follow: after them, Greek philosophy soon divided into four separate schools of thought: the cynics, skeptics, Epicureans, and stoics. The cynics followed the thinking—and eccentric lifestyle—of Diogenes of Sinope, who took Socrates's idea of rejecting conventional ideas of virtue to an extreme. Diogenes regarded desires for wealth, power, and honor as obstacles to virtue, preventing one from living a good and happy life. Instead, he advocated a simple life, free from material possessions, and in harmony with human nature. This was no mere philosophical stance; Diogenes lived on the streets of Athens with no home except a discarded ceramic tub, wearing rags, scrounging food, and ignoring the norms of social custom and etiquette. Like Socrates, he would accost Athenian citizens, but more critically; he was said to carry a lamp even in daylight "to help him find an honest man." He was nicknamed "the Dog" for his lifestyle, and the word *kynikos*, doglike, was adopted for the school of philosophy he founded.

Skeptics: Pyrrho and his followers

It is in the nature of philosophical inquiry for assumptions to be questioned, but Pyrrho and his followers, the skeptics, made doubt the central principle of their philosophy. Like Plato, they believed that human senses cannot be relied upon, and therefore that we cannot know how things are, only how they appear. Consequently any evidence we have for an assertion, since it comes from our senses, is equally unreliable. This does not mean that it is wrong, but that it could be wrong or right. In logical argument, this meant that the truth of the premises is in doubt and can only be established by arguments based on other unreliable premises, *ad infinitum*: there can be no ultimate certainty. So, they reasoned, for every assertion, a completely opposing and contradictory assertion can be made with equal justification. Skepticism can be seen as an extreme form of relativism, and in its purest form denies the validity of any philosophical argument. Despite this, it was to have a strong influence, especially on the philosophy of science and the logic-based philosophies of the 20th century.

Epicureans

Despite the connotations of its name today, there was more to the Epicurean school of philosophy than simple hedonism. Although its founder Epicurus saw the "good life" as the pursuit of fulfillment and happiness, he regarded the goal of life as peace of mind and freedom from fear—in particular, the preoccupying fear of death. Epicureanism was based on a belief that all matter, including our bodies, is composed of indestructible atoms. When we die, these are dispersed and re-form elsewhere; it is the end of our physical being and our consciousness, so is an end to both physical and emotional pain. Death, therefore, is nothing to be feared, and we should concentrate on enjoying life rather than fearing a nonexistent afterlife. Epicurus went further, questioning the relevance of gods, and even the existence of a benevolent god (although outright denial of the existence of god would have landed him in serious trouble). Inevitably, Epicureanism was quashed by later Christian and Islamic philosophies that followed, but many of its principles reappeared in modern scientific and liberal humanism.

Death ... is nothing to us, seeing that, when we are, death is not come, and, when death is come, we are not.

(Epicurus)

The immortal soul

Epicurus was probably the first philosopher to categorically deny that humans have an immortal soul. Working from the theory of atomism (see page 52), he believed that not only is everything composed of atoms, but also there is nothing else —everything is material, and our physical death is the end of our existence. This was, and continued to be, a minority opinion.

Until the Enlightenment, most philosophers took the view that the senses and reason were separate, residing in the body and soul respectively. Plato saw evidence for the soul's immortality in our innate knowledge of the world of Forms, which he suggested was remembered from previous existences. Aristotle also argued that although we gain knowledge through senses that disappear when our bodies die, the soul is responsible for our thoughts and can exist without a body; because it is immaterial, it cannot be corrupted and is therefore immortal. Belief in an immortal soul is essential to most religions, and a cornerstone of Eastern philosophy.

Stoics: philosophy of the Roman Empire

The last school of philosophy to emerge in ancient Greece, stoicism, evolved from the notion of virtue residing in simplicity and human nature proposed by the cynics. Zeno of Citium (not to be confused with Zeno of Elea, see page 46), founder of the stoic school, taught that nature is the only reality, and that we are a part of it. Using our capacity for reason, we must learn to accept things we have no control over and also to control our destructive emotions. Virtue alone is sufficient to ensure the happiness of a "good life," and anybody who has knowledge of virtue and leads a virtuous life will not be affected by any misfortunes that befall him. The development of stoic philosophy coincided with the decline of Greek political and cultural influence and the rise of Roman power. The Romans, not previously known for their enthusiasm for philosophy, found stoicism fitted comfortably with their own culture of ethics, and it became the prevailing philosophy of the Roman Empire, adopted by thinkers including Seneca, Epictetus, and Marcus Aurelius.

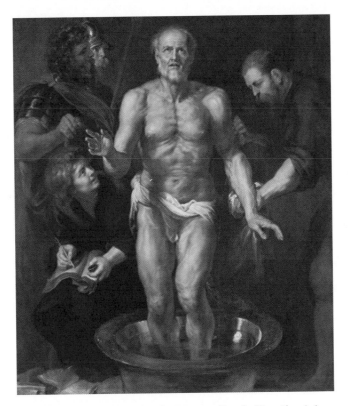

Ordered to commit suicide by the Emperor Nero in 65 CE, the stoic philosopher Seneca met his end with typical sobriety.

Eastern philosophy

Until quite recently, Western philosophy developed in isolation from the traditions of China and India. The division between religion and philosophy was less clear-cut in the East, where adherence to a religion involved acceptance of its moral philosophy, and philosophy assumed belief in a religious, or at least unsupported, metaphysical explanation. The first great Eastern philosophers, such as Laozi and Confucius in China and Siddhartha Gautama in India, were roughly contemporary with the first Greek philosophers, but their emphasis on morals anticipated Athenian philosophy. In some respects, their conclusions were strikingly similar, but with the arrival of Christianity, Eastern and Western philosophies became marked by differences rather than similarities. In the 19th century, some Western philosophers "discovered" Indian religion and philosophy, and realized the similarity to the views of German idealism in particular. More recently, the religious aspects of Eastern philosophies have taken precedence, while philosophical thinking in the East has come under Western influences.

Daoism

One of the primary concerns for the dynastic states of China in the sixth century BCE was to establish a system of government that reflected traditional religious ideas. A class of scholars with civic responsibilities had emerged, and among them was Laozi (or Lao Tzu), who proposed a comprehensive moral philosophy as a basis for social and political organization. This view of the world subsequently became known as Daosim. Laozi started from a belief that the ever-changing world was made up of complementary states: light and dark, night and day, life and death, each arising from the other in a cyclical fashion and in eternal harmony and balance. These "10,000 manifestations" form the process of change known as *dao*, "the way," characterized by "not-being" and beyond human understanding. We disturb the cosmic balance if we stray from the *dao* by giving in to desire, ambition, or social convention; to live in accordance with the *dao*, we must adopt a life of "nonaction," a simple and tranquil life in harmony with nature, behaving intuitively and thoughtfully, not impulsively.

The Chinese character for Dao, "the way," used as a symbol of Daoism.

Confucianism

Kong Fuzi, known in the West as Confucius, was of the generation following Laozi, and may have consulted him in his capacity as court archivist. While Laozi had outlined a moral philosophy, Confucius was concerned with providing a political structure that would allow a stable but just government. This, he argued, should be based on virtue and benevolence but, contrary to conventional belief, he thought moral goodness was not god-given, nor restricted to any particular social class. Instead, he believed that virtue could be cultivated, and that it was the ruling class's role to lead by example. The *junzi*, or "superior man," by making his virtue manifest, would inspire virtue in others, which could be reinforced by ceremony, ritual, and social niceties. This could best be achieved by a hierarchical society in which faithfulness was the guiding principle: a ruler should be benevolent, and in return his subjects would show loyalty. Confucius extended this reciprocal faithfulness to other relationships—between loving parent and obedient child, husband and wife, siblings, and friends and colleagues.

The Golden Rule

The idea of reciprocal respect as a model for human relationships is central to the moral philosophy of Confucius (see page 110). He also advocated reciprocity as a guide for our behavior toward others: "what you do not desire for yourself, do not do to others." Interestingly, Confucius presents this "ethic of reciprocity" in a negative form (as do many Eastern religions), implying restraint rather than action, while in the West it is more familiar as the positive "do unto others as you would have them do unto you." In one form or another, this maxim has featured in almost all major religions, and has been stated by many moral philosophers. Because of its universal acceptance, it has become known as the "Golden Rule."

This concept is not only fundamental to ideas of ethics, but also has implications for political philosophy. Incorporating the principle into a system of government raises questions of how much its rule should impinge upon the lives of its citizens—how authoritarian or libertarian it should be.

JUDAISM

"Love thy neighbor as thyself."

BUDDHISM

"Hurt not others with that which pains yourself."

CHRISTIANITY

"Whatever you wish people would do unto you, so do unto them."

HINDUISM

"People should always treat others as they themselves wish to be treated."

Samsara, dharma, karma, and moksha

Many different religious traditions arose among the early civilizations of India, but most had certain concepts in common. Now known collectively as Hinduism, these religions shared a belief in reincarnation—a cycle of birth, life, death, and rebirth, called *samsara*. Along with this came a belief that liberation from this cycle can be achieved by leading a good life, so that a moral philosophy was an intrinsic part of religion.

The immortal soul, *atman*, is reborn in many forms according to *karma*, the moral law that rules the universe and determines action and reaction. The ultimate aim of life is *moksha*, release from the cycle of birth and rebirth, by devotion to God, but also through knowledge of *karma*, and especially through *dharma*, appropriate action. The idea of *dharma*, the duties and ethics necessary for leading a good life, provided a complete moral philosophy in many ways similar to that of the Greek philosophers, but inextricably connected with a religious explanation of the universe.

The Hindu Dharmacakra, or "wheel of life," symbolizes *dharma*, the path to enlightenment.

Buddhism

Siddhartha Gautama, later known as the Buddha, was born in India in the sixth-century BCE and brought up in the religious tradition of belief in a cycle of birth and rebirth. He gave up his comfortable background and adopted an austere lifestyle in a quest for release from this cycle, but realized this was not leading to a life of fulfillment either. He reasoned there was a "middle way" between the extremes of sensual pleasure and asceticism (anticipating the idea of the Golden Mean, see page 90). Life is characterized by suffering, caused by unfulfillable desires. We can avoid this suffering by overcoming our egos and giving up "attachments" to worldly power and possessions. He summed this idea up in the Four Noble Truths: those of suffering, of the origin of suffering, of the end of suffering, and of the "Eightfold Path" to the end of suffering. By following the Eightfold Path (right mindfulness, right action, right intention, right livelihood, right effort, right concentration, right speech, and right understanding), we can lead a life of fulfillment and escape the cycle of rebirth to achieve a state of *nirvana*.

Christianity and philosophy

The doctrines of the Christian Church dominated the philosophy of medieval Europe. Christianity, especially in its early period, placed less emphasis on philosophical reasoning and more on faith and authority. Philosophy was regarded with suspicion, and the ideas of the Greek philosophers were initially considered incompatible with Christian belief. The Church had a virtual monopoly on scholarship, but some Christian thinkers introduced elements of Greek philosophy, especially that of Plato and Aristotle. After careful examination by the authorities, many of these were gradually integrated into doctrine. From the end of the Roman Empire to the 15th century, a distinct Christian philosophy evolved, starting with Augustine and culminating in the comprehensive philosophy of Thomas Aquinas. With the Renaissance, however, the authority of the Church, and the papacy in particular, was challenged by a resurgence of humanist views. Scientific discoveries contradicted core beliefs, and the invention of printing meant the Church could no longer control access to information.

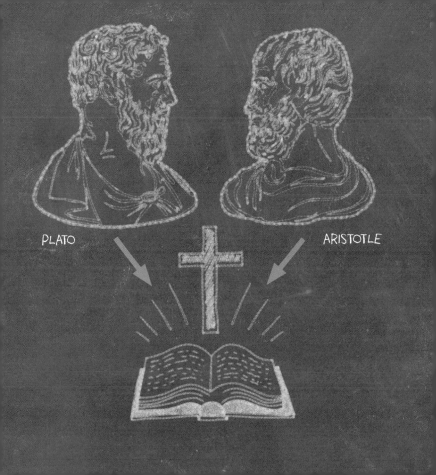

PLATO

ARISTOTLE

Reconciling faith and reason

The first significant Christian philosopher was Augustine of Hippo. Although his mother was a Christian, he at first rejected the faith and studied philosophy, flirting for a while with the Persian religion of Manichaeism. It was only after a thorough study of Greek philosophy, and especially Plato and the "Neo-Platonism" taught by Plotinus, that he converted. Unsurprisingly, his approach to Christianity was colored by his philosophy. He believed the two were not incompatible: Christianity is characterized by belief, philosophy by reasoning but, he argued, faith and reason can not only coexist, but are complementary. He suggested that Christianity could absorb the philosophy of Plato without contradicting any of its central beliefs, in order to provide a rational basis for its theology. His work coincided with the adoption of Christianity as the official religion of the Roman Empire, and in his book *The City of God* he explained how it was possible to be a citizen of an earthly community at the same time as living in the eternal and true world of the kingdom of God—an idea adapted from Platonism.

St. Augustine was a key figure in both the history of Western philosophy and the development of Christianity.

Existence of God: the teleological argument

A recurrent concern for medieval Christianity was whether there could be a philosophical, rational proof of God's existence. While many in the Church believed this to be simply a matter of faith, the incorporation of philosophy into religion encouraged rational justification. Several arguments for God's existence were put forward, including the so-called argument of design, or teleological argument (from the Greek *telos*, purpose). The reasoning goes that if we look at the world around us, we see evidence of order. Everything looks as if it has been designed for a purpose, and if everything has been designed, then there must have been a designer—God. The argument, developed from ideas in Plato and Aristotle, appears not only in Christian philosophers such as Augustine and Thomas Aquinas, but also in the work of the Islamic philosopher Averroes (see page 160). Later philosophers challenged this, questioning the notion of purpose and replacing it with cause, while scientific advances, in particular the theory of evolution, have helped to refute the argument.

William Blake's
The Ancient of Days
depicts God as an
all-powerful
architect of the
universe.

The problem of evil

Christian philosophers not only sought a rational argument *for* the existence of God, but also had to deal with opposing arguments. One of the most powerful, proposed by Epicurus, raises the problem of the existence of evil. In the Epicurean paradox, he asks: "Is God willing to prevent evil, but not able? Then he is not omnipotent. Is he able, but not willing? Then he is malevolent. Is he both able and willing? Then why is there evil in the world? Is he neither able nor willing? Then why call him God?"

Augustine, the first Christian philosopher to address this paradox, argued that God gives us the freedom to choose whether to do right or wrong. Although God created everything that exists, he did not create evil, as evil is not a thing but a lack—a deficiency of good that came about as a result of man's rationality, given to us when Adam chose to eat the fruit of the tree of knowledge. Evil is therefore the price we pay for God allowing us free will—although this in itself raises further questions of God's omniscience.

John Milton's *Paradise Lost* explores the notions of evil and free will through the story of the fallen angel Satan.

Free will vs. determinism

According to Christian belief, God allowed Adam the freedom to choose whether to eat the forbidden fruit. Although He is omnipotent, He has given us free will to decide our actions. But He is also omniscient. And if He knows what we are going to do, then our actions must be predestined, so how can we be said to have free will? The early Christian philosopher Boethius answered this by explaining that God's knowledge of our future actions does not prevent us from being free to make a choice. God foresees, but does not control, our thoughts and actions.

This problem has continued to occupy philosophers. On the one hand, there is determinism, the belief that everything that happens is determined by conditions so that nothing else *could* happen; on the other, the libertarian belief that we are free to choose our actions, and free will and determinism are incompatible. Somewhere in between are those who believe that our *choices* are determined but our decisions are our own—we are free to play the hand that we are dealt.

The Consolation
of Philosophy

Around 524 CE, the Roman philosopher Boethius offered his thoughts on the problem of free will (see page 126) in his book *The Consolation of Philosophy,* written while he was in prison awaiting execution on charges of treason. He presents his ideas as a conversation with Philosophy personified, who offers her wisdom to console him. They discuss virtue, justice, and human nature, as well as free will and predestination—the same subjects that concerned classical Greek philosophers.

Boethius was a Christian, and the book deals with many matters of faith, but it is significant that he found consolation in philosophy rather than religion. At this period, Christianity was beginning to assimilate philosophical ideas into its doctrine —philosophers such as Augustine and Boethius represented both the end of classical philosophy and the beginning of this process. That there was a place for philosophy in Christianity was confirmed by the continued influence of Boethius's work throughout the Middle Ages and into the Renaissance.

Boethius and his students depicted in an illuminated
manuscript copy of *The Consolation of Philosophy*.

Scholasticism and dogma

The Catholic Church wielded considerable social and political power in medieval Europe, and also controlled access to learning. Education was provided by the Church and necessarily followed Christian doctrine, while libraries and universities were funded by the Church and staffed by monastic orders. Monks preserved and translated many ancient texts, mostly of Greek philosophy and latterly acquired from Islamic scholars. Scholasticism was a method of tuition that used rigorous dialectical reasoning both to teach Christian theology and to scrutinize these texts. Clerics and academics used methods of reasoning developed by Plato and Aristotle to assess the compatibility of ideas with Christian doctrine. The theories of philosophers including Augustine and Thomas Aquinas were also examined, and either adopted to defend Christian dogma or dismissed as heretical. Scholasticism played an important part in the integration of philosophical ideas into Christianity, remaining the predominant ethos for Christian education and theology until supplanted by humanist ideas in the Renaissance.

Abelard and Universals

Today, Peter Abelard is best known for his illicit love affair and secret marriage to Heloise, which brought about the end of his academic career. But this overshadows his role as one of the most influential Christian thinkers of the 11th century. Abelard was a prominent scholastic philosopher, well versed in Aristotelian logic. He shared Aristotle's rigorously systematic character, and was skeptical about the Platonism that had become absorbed into Christianity. The prevailing view, realism, was based on Plato's theory of Forms (see page 72), and maintained that the properties things have in common—the "blueness" of both a garden cornflower and the sea, for example—exist independently as "Universals." Abelard, however, took Aristotle's view that the common property is inherent in its particular instances, and argued that the Universal only exists in our thoughts—a concept, not a reality. His theory, which became known as conceptualism, initially met with opposition, but spearheaded a movement to incorporate the ideas of Aristotle, as well as Plato, into Christian theology.

Oranges, balls, and planets all exhibit the Universal "roundness."

Existence of God:
the ontological argument

With the rise of scholasticism and Christianity's embrace of Aristotelian logic in the 11th century came a renewed interest in reconciling matters of faith with reasoned argument. One of the founding fathers of the scholastic movement was Saint Anselm, best known for proposing the so-called ontological argument for the existence of God.

Anselm asks us to imagine the most perfect being possible. If such a being does not exist, however, it cannot be the most perfect possible and must be inferior to one of the same perfection that does exist. So, the most perfect being possible must exist—in Anselm's words, "God is that, than which nothing greater can be conceived." As a logical argument, however, this is flawed, and contemporaries such as Gaunilo of Marmoutiers pointed out that it could be used to prove the existence of anything. Later philosophers, notably Thomas Aquinas and later Immanuel Kant, showed that while the argument presented a notion of God's essence, it was no proof of His existence.

God is the greatest thing in the universe.

But what if God doesn't exist?

In that case, He's not really that great ...

So if he's really the greatest thing in the universe, then he *must* exist!

Pascal's wager

Today, it is generally agreed that there can be no logical proof either way for the existence of God, and that this is purely a matter of faith. Philosophical speculation on the subject, however, continued well into the so-called "Age of Reason." One novel take on the problem was raised by the mathematician Blaise Pascal in the 17th century. "Pascal's wager" examines whether, given that we can have no proof of His existence, it is a better bet to believe in God or not. Pascal weighs up the pros and cons in terms of the consequences: if God exists and I deny his existence, I run the risk of eternal damnation; if He exists and I accept His existence, I earn eternal life in paradise; but if He doesn't exist, it will make no difference to me. On balance, then, it is a safer bet to believe in His existence. Although Pascal's wager is an interesting exercise in logic and rudimentary game theory, it is based on some shaky premises—we are asked to assume that God bases His decision on my afterlife on my belief in Him, that He, too, is a rational being and that heaven and hell also exist.

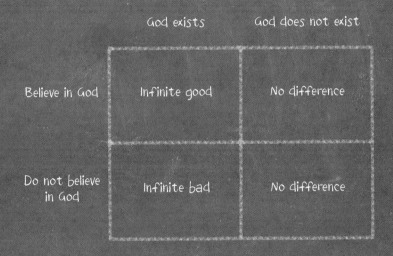

	God exists	God does not exist
Believe in God	Infinite good	No difference
Do not believe in God	Infinite bad	No difference

Thomas Aquinas

Probably the greatest of medieval Christian philosophers, Thomas Aquinas's major achievement was to synthesize the apparently contradictory philosophies of Plato and Aristotle and show they were complementary to Christian belief. From Plato's view of Universals in his theory of Forms (see page 72), he derived the notion of what he called the essence of things. This, he said, was distinct from its existence: for example, it is possible to describe the attributes of a dragon—its essence—yet still deny its existence. He further argued that since God created everything according to his design, the essence of things must precede their existence. But he also believed that our minds are like a clean slate, or *tabula rasa*, and took from Aristotle the idea that we acquire knowledge through our senses. While careful to distinguish such ideas from questions of faith, Aquinas did not see them as incompatible. These rational explanations concern the way we learn about the world, but we can still believe it to be God's creation. Inevitably, it took some time for such ideas to be accepted by the Church.

Existence of God: the cosmological argument

Thomas Aquinas used his ideas of essence and existence to refute Anselm's ontological argument for the existence of God (see page 134). Instead, he proposed a stronger argument, known as the cosmological argument, derived from Aristotle's notion of causes (see page 86). In brief, he argued that something must have caused the universe to exist, a First Cause, and this is what we call God. As explanation, Aquinas says that although the universe obviously exists, it is conceivable that in other circumstances it might not exist; its existence is therefore contingent on a cause. This has to be something that cannot conceivably *not exist*, and is not contingent on anything else—an uncaused cause. This, Aquinas says, we understand to be God. The similarity of the cosmological argument to the scientific Big Bang theory is striking, and both involve the philosophically problematic acceptance of a first, uncaused, cause. However, refuting it by denying the possibility of an uncaused cause involves the equally difficult problem of infinite regress (see page 36).

Natural Law

Christian philosophers could base their moral philosophy on the teaching of Jesus, but extending this to political philosophy raised the question of how far the laws of man were compatible with the law of God. Augustine tackled the issue in *The City of God* (see page 120), contrasting earthly society and the kingdom of God in a similar way to Plato's worlds of appearances and Forms. Taking the idea further, Thomas Aquinas suggested that human laws were separate from God's eternal laws but that there also exists a Natural Law, based on human behavior, morals, and virtues, that is a part of God's law.

An important part of Natural Law was the concept of "Just War." Christianity (and many other religions) preaches pacifism, but politics sometimes makes war necessary. Rather than being a contradiction of God's law, however, Aquinas suggested that war could be justified by Natural Law. Again basing his ideas on Augustine, he proposed three requirements for war to be just: rightful intention, a just cause, and authority of the sovereign.

Acts and omissions

In common usage, "ethics" refers to how we judge the morality of our actions. At the heart of any judgment we make of an action are two things: the consequences of that action, and the intention of the person making it. While the seriousness of the consequences provokes our immediate reaction, with further thought we realize that intention is crucial to deciding morality. Is a deliberate theft less morally defensible than a fatal mistake? Moral judgment is simple when both intention and consequences are bad, but not so easy to decide when serious consequences are a result of good intentions, or at least without bad intention.

Further dilemmas arise when deliberate choices have to be made. Sometimes a sacrifice has to be made for "the greater good"; there are cases where several lives can be saved by the deliberate loss of another, for instance. But do the ends always justify the means? And is there a moral difference between deliberate action and deliberately allowing something to happen?

A runaway train (1) is out of control and hurtling toward a final set of switches (2). Should the signalman take action by diverting the train onto a sideline where a group of workmen will be killed (3), or is he morally less culpable if he takes no action and allows the train to speed on and ultimately crash in the station (4), killing many more people?

Nominalism

Because Plato's philosophy had been firmly assimilated into Christian doctrine from the time of Augustine, the introduction of Aristotle's contrasting ideas met with some resistance. Scholastic philosophers adopted a rigorous Aristotelian methodology, but his views on the problem of Universals (see page 132) were seen as contradicting Church teachings. Peter Abelard was among the first to challenge the idea of realism (that the Universals have a real, independent existence) with his idea of conceptualism (that they exist only in our minds). Thirteenth-century philosophers such as John Duns Scotus and William of Ockham went further, arguing that the Universals did not exist *at all*, except as names referring to properties of things in the real world. Unlike Aquinas's synthesis (see page 138), this "nominalist" idea directly contradicted realism. Christian philosophy split into opposing schools of thought on the issue—a division echoing differences between Plato and Aristotle, which persisted well beyond the Renaissance between continental rationalists and British empiricists.

Jean DUNS dit SCOT.
nommé le Docteur subtil Religieux de
l'ordre de St Francois né en Ecosse et
mort a Cologne en 1308. agé de 35. ans.

For Duns Scotus, the Universals were simply adjectives used to describe the properties of real-world objects.

Ockham's razor and Buridan's ass

William of Ockham wrote widely on scientific subjects and logic as well as philosophy and theology. He maintained a distinction between matters of faith and what we would now call science, but was eventually excommunicated from the Church for heresy. Influenced by Aristotle, he believed in using the evidence of observation and experience as a basis for rational arguments, anticipating the later "scientific method."

He is perhaps best known for the principle known as Ockham's razor: when there are two alternative explanations for something, all things being equal, the simpler explanation is more likely to be correct. We should "shave off" unnecessary assumptions and choose the explanation with the fewest causes, factors, or variables. Ockham's pupil Jean Buridan lent his name to a different paradox of rational choice between alternatives. Buridan's ass is a hungry beast placed exactly halfway between two equally attractive bales of hay. Unable to choose between the two, it eventually starves to death.

When faced with two equally convincing arguments, we run the risk of choosing neither, when in fact it makes no difference so long as we make a decision.

Learned ignorance

Aristotle's methodical, empiricist philosophy only gradually became integrated into Christianity in the late Middle Ages (see page 146). Part of the problem was that the Aristotelian approach, using the evidence of our senses and subjecting it to logical reasoning, was too down to earth and detracted from the mystical elements of religion. Realism, with its idea of another, perfect world of Universals, fitted better with Christian concepts such as the Trinity. In reaction to this almost scientific approach, some clung doggedly to Plato's ideas. Nicholas of Cusa (also known as Cusanus, or Nicolaus von Kues) went even further, proposing a "learned ignorance" reminiscent of Socrates. All our knowledge, he said, comes from what he called "the One," or "the Good," and God, who came before everything, necessarily came before that. It is therefore impossible to have any knowledge of God with the human mind. We can only use our reason to understand that we *cannot* know God, and through this "learned ignorance" access the divine mind to comprehend God.

Erasmus and humanism

Toward the end of the 15th century, political power was shifting from the Roman Catholic Church to secular nation-states. Intellectuals had become less interested in theology and concerned themselves more with earthly matters. This new emphasis on "humanism" had an effect even within the the Church. Medieval scholasticism had sought to reconcile rational philosophical thinking with Christian theology, but there was a growing feeling that the two should be kept separate—philosophy is based on reason, but religion on faith.

Dutch philosopher Desiderius Erasmus, however, took on board the humanist emphasis on the individual, arguing that an individual's relationship with God was more relevant than Catholic doctrine. He suggested that the values of simplicity, naivety, and humility advocated by the Christian scriptures are fundamentally human traits. Knowledge, especially of the kind discussed by philosophy, is an obstacle to leading the "good life" exemplified by Jesus, and a hindrance to faith.

Reformation: undermining authority

The authority of the Church came under increasing pressure as secular Renaissance humanism spread across Europe. Papal authority was challenged by new secular rulers and governments, and advances in scientific discovery contradicted Catholic dogma. But it was not only pressure from outside the Church that brought about change; many within saw the Church as corrupt and remote from the people, especially in northern Europe. Martin Luther's *Ninety-five Theses*, a tirade against clerical abuses posted in 1517, sparked the Protestant Reformation and created a schism in the Church that was symptomatic of the mood of the time. With the invention of printing, access to information moved beyond the control of the Catholic Church, and the domination of medieval scholastic philosophy came to an end. The new humanist ideas were manifested at first in the cultural and artistic movement of the Renaissance, but also provided fertile ground for science and philosophy, culminating in the 18th-century "Age of Reason" that marked the beginning of modern philosophy and science.

ueritatis hæc subscripta disputabunt Vuittenbergæ, Præsidéte
R.P. Martino Luther, Artiu & S. Theologiæ Magistro, eius
deinq; ibidem lectore Ordinario. Quare petit ut qui non pos
sunt uerbis præsentes nobiscum disceptare, agant id literis ab-
sentes. In nomine domini nostri Iesu Christi. Amen.

i   Minus & Magister noster Iesus Christus, di-
cendo pœnitentiā agite &c. omnem uitam fi
delium, pœnitentiam esse uoluit.

ij   Quod uerbū pœnitentiæ de pœnitentia sacra-
mentali,(.i. confessionis & satisfactionis quæ
sacerdotum ministerio celebratur) non potest intelligi.

iij   Non tamen solā intédit interiorē; immo interior nulla est, nisi
foris operetur uarias carnis mortificationes.

iiij   Manet itaq; pœna donec manet odium sui,(.i. pœnitentia uera
intus) scilicet usq; ad introitum regni cælorum.

v   Papa non uult nec potest, ullas pœnas remittere; præter eas,
quas arbitrio uel suo uel canonum imposuit.

vj   Papa nō potest remittere ullam culpā, nisi declarādo & appro
bando remissam a deo. Aut certe remittédo casus reseruatos
sibi, quibus contéptis culpa prorsus remaneret.

vij   Nulli prorsus remittit deus culpam, quin simul eum subijciat
humiliatum in omnibus sacerdoti suo uicario.

viij   Canones pœnitentiales solū uiuentibus sunt impositi; nihilq;
morituris, secundū eosdem debet imponi.

ix   Inde bene nobis facit spiritussanctus in Papa: excipiédo in su-
is decretis semper articulum mortis & necessitatis.

x   Indoctè & male faciūt sacerdotes ij, qui morituris pœnitétias
canonicas in purgatorium reseruant.

xj   Zizania illa de mutanda pœna Canonica in pœnā purgatorij, uidentur certe dormientibus Episcopis seminata.

xij   Olim pœnæ canonicæ nō post, sed ante absolutionem impo-
nebantur, tanq; tentamenta ueræ contritionis.

xiij   Morituri, per mortem omnia soluunt, & legibus canonū mor-
tui iam sunt, habentes iure earū relaxationem.

xiiij   Imperfecta sanitas seu charitas morituri, necessario secum fert
magnū timorem, táq; maiorē, quáto minor fuerit ipsa.

xv   Hic timor & horror, satis est, se solo(ut alia taceam) facere pœ-
nam purgatorij, cum sit proximus desperationis horrori.

xvj   Videntur infernus, purgatorium, cælum differre; sicut desperatio, prope desperatio, securitas differunt.

xvij   Necessarium uidetur animabus in purgatorio sicut minui hor
rorem, ita augeri charitatem.

xviij   Nec probatū uidetur ullis, aut rationibus, aut scripturis, q sint
extra statum meriti seu augendæ charitatis.

xix   Nec hoc probatū esse uidetur, q sint de sua beatitudine certæ
& securæ, saltem ōs, licet nos certissimi simus.

xx   Igitur Papa per remissionē plenariā omniū pœnarū, non simpli
citer omniū intelligit, sed a seipso tmmodo impositarū.

xxj   Errant itaq; indulgentiarū prædicatores ij, qui dicunt per Pa-
pæ indulgentias, hominē ab omni pœna solui & saluari.

xxij   Quin nullam remittit animabus in purgatorio, quā in hac ui-
ta debuissent secundum Canones soluere.

xxiij   Si remissio ulla omniū omnino pœnarū pōt alicui dari; certū
est eam nō nisi perfectissimis,.i. paucissimis dari.

xxiiij   Falli ob id necesse est, maiorem parté populi; per indifferenté
illam & magnificam pœnæ solutæ promissionem.

xxv   Qualē potestaté habet Papa i purgatoriū gñaliter talé habet
q̃libet Episcopus & curatꝰ in sua diœcesi, & parochia spaliter.

i   Optime facit Papa, q̃ nō potestate clauis (quā nullam habet)
sed per modum suffragij, dat animabus remissionem.

ij   Hominē prædicant, qui statim, ut iactus nūmus in cistam tin-
nierit, euolare dicunt animam.

iij   Certū est nūmo in cistam tinniente, augeri quæstum & auari-
ciam posse; suffragiū aūt ecclesiæ est in arbitrio dei solius.

iiij   Quis scit si omnes animæ in purgatorio uelint redimi, sicut de
sancto Seuerino & paschali factum narratur?

v   Nullus securus est de ueritate suæ contritionis; multo minus

An extract from Luther's *Ninety-five Theses*.

Philosophy and Islam

Following its foundation by Mohammed in the seventh century, Islam spread rapidly from Arabia into Asia, across northern Africa, and even to southern Spain. The Islamic Empire rivaled Christian Europe in size and influence, and its stability produced a flourishing culture. The Islamic "Golden Age" began around 750 CE and lasted for more than five centuries. Islam encouraged scholarship and, unlike the Christianity of the time, recognized that religion and rational inquiry could exist side by side.

Islamic scholars, often polymaths educated in science and philosophy as well as theology, preserved and translated Greek texts (most notably the works of Aristotle), but also scientific and mathematical works from India. As a result, scholars made advances in fields such as astronomy, medicine, mathematics, and alchemy that would not have been possible in the Christian world. A distinctive Islamic "school" of philosophy evolved, and two great figures, Avicenna and Averroes, incorporated the ideas of Plato and Aristotle into Islamic theology.

Avicenna and the flying man

Aristotelian philosophy and science thrived during the Islamic "Golden Age," Baghdad and Damascus in particular became centers of intellectual activity, attracting philosopher-scientists including al-Kindi and al-Farabi. In Persia, Ibn Sina, known in the West as Avicenna, was known as a pioneering physician, but also an important philosopher and theologian. Although he had studied Aristotle, he was also influenced by Plato and the idea of dualism—that there is a realm of immaterial things separate from the world we live in. Avicenna developed the idea of dualism further, arguing that our senses and reason, corresponding to our body and mind, are similarly distinct. He illustrated this with the image of a "flying man," blindfolded and floating in the air, effectively deprived of all his senses. Despite receiving no information from his senses, he is still aware that he has a "self" or "soul" that exists but has no physical substance. The mind and body coexist, but are distinct; the mind or soul exists in the realm of immaterial things and so is not destroyed when the physical body dies.

Averroes

In the 11th and 12th centuries, Avicenna's Neo-Platonist take on Aristotle's ideas was the dominant philosophy of Islam, but it was not without critics. Hard-line theologians such as al-Ghazali saw Aristotelianism as contrary to the Qur'an, but his objections triggered a reaction that ironically strengthened the influence of Aristotle in Islamic philosophy. Al-Ghazali's staunchest opponent was Ibn Rushd (Latinized as Averroes), from Islamic southern Iberia. As well as refuting al-Ghazali's arguments, he dismissed many of Avicenna's Plato-inspired ideas, advocating Aristotle's own far more empirical and rational approach. He argued that there was no incompatibility between religion and philosophy: the Qur'an presents a poetic, metaphorical truth that can be interpreted with philosophical reasoning. However, he believed this should only be done by suitably educated scholars—an idea paradoxically similar to those of Plato. Although his ideas aroused some controversy, translations of his work had a significant influence on the Christian scholastic philosophy of medieval Europe.

Islamic influence on
Western philosophy

Islamic philosophy grew largely from the Greek tradition, with philosophers such as Averroes and Avicenna adding their own commentaries to the ideas of Plato and Aristotle. Many of these philosophers worked in the universities and libraries of the major Islamic cities, notably the Bayt al-Hikma or "House of Wisdom" in Baghdad, where ancient texts were preserved and translated. This was in contrast with Christian scholarship, which remained suspicious of what it saw as pagan philosophy. In the 11th century, however, Christian conquests of Jerusalem, Sicily, and some of Islamic Spain increased contact between the two cultures. European scholars gained access to the ancient texts and their Islamic commentaries, translating them into Latin. The new availability of classical ideas prompted a renewed interest in philosophy in Christian Europe, and the works of Aristotle in particular became the foundation of the scholastic movement (see page 130). Just as importantly, Islamic scientific and mathematical ideas became available—although it took much longer for their influence to become noticeable.

The Greek mathematical, scientific, and philosophical knowledge that enriched Islamic culture was virtually unknown in Europe until the 11th century.

Renaissance, reason, and revolution

After about a millennium of control, the Catholic Church lost its stranglehold on European cultural and intellectual life in the Renaissance, allowing philosophers to turn their attention to more humanistic concerns. The emergence of new secular powers aroused a renewed interest in political philosophy. At the same time, science (in the guise of "natural philosophy") gradually asserted its own authority. Nicolaus Copernicus's 1543 assertion that Earth was not the stationary center of the universe was just the beginning of a scientific revolution overturning ecclesiastical dogma. The subsequent work of scientists such as Galileo and Francis Bacon paved the way for a more systematic method that influenced all aspects of science and philosophy. This led to the so-called Age of Reason, or Enlightenment, of the 17th and 18th centuries, producing the great schools of thought that set the agenda for philosophy in the modern era: rationalism in mainland Europe and empiricism in Britain—but also the political philosophies that led to the establishment of modern democracies.

Copernicus's idea of a heliocentric universe undermined the authority of the Church and marked the beginning of a scientific revolution.

Renaissance humanism

Beginning in 14th-century Florence, the Renaissance was a "rebirth" of classical Greek and Latin culture in Europe after more than a millennium of dominance by the Catholic Church. Prompted by the rediscovery of classical texts, the movement placed humans rather than God at the center of attention. While Copernicus, Galileo, and Kepler attempted to understand the structure of the universe (harking back to the concerns of the first philosophers), Vesalius and Leonardo da Vinci examined human anatomy in meticulous detail. The Renaissance was primarily a cultural and artistic movement, but its emphasis on humanism influenced political thought and was reflected in the foundation of republics such as Florence and Venice. Here, Renaissance ideals flourished, aided by the invention of printing and the trade that replaced medieval feudalism. Humanism had enormous influence on later philosophy but, with the notable exception of political philosophers such as Machiavelli and reformers in the Church, it was science, not philosophy, that took center stage at the time.

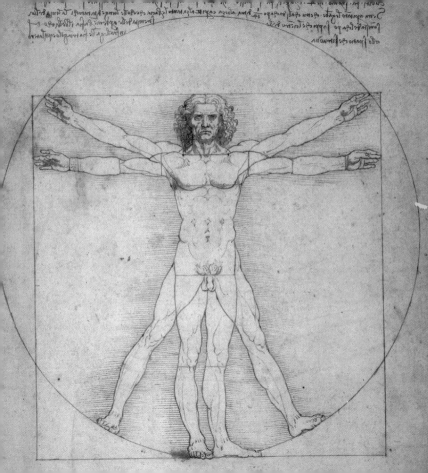

Machiavelli and political realism

Florence is widely regarded as the birthplace of the cultural movement that characterized the Renaissance, but it was also one of the first Italian republics and, thanks to the ensuing tensions between Church and state, home to intrigue and political chicanery. Against this background emerged the first modern, secular political philosopher—Niccolò Machiavelli. His book *The Prince*, ostensibly a handbook of advice on how to gain and exercise power, was also a realistic description of politics.

Machiavelli argued that it is fruitless to theorize about an ideal political society, distinguishing between private individual morality and the expediency of the ruler and state. A ruler, he says, must at times be prepared to act immorally, using violence and deceit if necessary: "consider the results that have been achieved ... rather than the means by which they have been executed." Machiavelli was, however, a republican at heart, and it is likely that *The Prince* was a satirical description of, in Francis Bacon's words, "what men do, not what they ought to do."

Ends and means

One of the implicit messages of the political realism in Machiavelli's *The Prince* was that "the end justifies the means." This marked a significant shift in political philosophy, and subsequently in moral philosophy as a whole, to judging an action's morality on its consequences rather than intentions or motives. As a result of Renaissance humanism, morally correct conduct was no longer dictated by religious authority, and ideas of good and evil were not as absolute as those of Christian doctrine. Political philosophy could similarly not be based on an ideal structure for society. Consequentialism, the notion that results are the basis for judging the rightness of conduct, became a prevalent approach in moral philosophy from the Renaissance into the Enlightenment, influencing the utilitarianism of the late 18th and early 19th centuries (see page 250). It was not until Immanuel Kant proposed his deontological (duty-based) system of moral philosophy (see page 264) that emphasis shifted from consequences to motives and intentions as a basis for moral judgments.

Was the Allied use of
atomic bombs in 1945
justified as a means of
accelerating the end of
the Second World War?

Moral luck

Modern philosophers have identified a problem with the idea of judging the rightness of an action by either its consequences or the motives behind it. Circumstances beyond our control can and do affect the outcome of our actions, often dramatically. Actions taken with the best of intentions may result in disaster, and it is not easy to judge the morality of, for example, a seemingly harmless prank that causes injury, or conversely a self-serving act that unintentionally brings prosperity to others. We may also blame or criticize actions that result from circumstances different from our own, such as the inhumanity of slave-owners, without knowing how any of us would have behaved in the same situation.

Moral judgment turns out to be far more complex than the simple assessment of consequences or even motives, raising questions such as what part chance plays in determining if an action is good or bad—is there such a thing as "moral luck"? And is it bad to be unlucky, or even unlucky to be bad?

Is a drunk-driver who kills someone in a crash morally worse than one who by chance happens not to?

Bacon and the scientific method

Part of the legacy of the Islamic "Golden Age" in European thought was a wealth of scientific scholarship, based on Aristotelian ideas of observation, analysis, and classification, but with a distinctively Islamic tradition of experimentation, especially in fields such as medicine and alchemy. During the Renaissance, European scientists adopted these principles, leading to significant advances in astronomy, mathematics, and the biological sciences. A turning point came, however, at the beginning of the 17th century with Francis Bacon's *Novum Organum*. Rather than simply continuing the tradition, this English philosopher examined the method of scientific inquiry itself, and proposed a more systematic approach. Bacon advocated a process of observation, amassing and analysis of data, formation of a hypothesis, and confirmation through critical experiments. This process of induction—deriving a general rule from a series of instances, forms the basis of modern scientific practice, and Bacon's insistence on evidence also influenced the British empiricist movement (see page 212).

Frontispiece of Bacon's great work, the *Novum Organum*.

A state of nature

As well as its flourishing culture, Renaissance Europe was marked by attempts to find a new political order to replace medieval feudalism. Independent states—republics as well as monarchies—emerged, and there was a renewed interest in how these should be governed. In England, the monarchy was overthrown in a civil war, but was restored after a short-lived republican Commonwealth as a "constitutional monarchy," subject to the consent of Parliament. During this revolutionary period, Thomas Hobbes wrote *Leviathan*, an examination of the nature of society and government. No doubt influenced by the horrors of civil war, he argued that in what he called a "state of nature," without political order, unlimited freedom allows everyone to act in their own self-interest. Each person is pitted against others in a constant battle for survival, and life is "solitary, poor, nasty, brutish, and short." The solution, he argued, is the formation of civil societies, in which people agree under a "social contract" to subject themselves to the rule of a sovereign in return for security and prosperity.

Frontispiece of Hobbes's *Leviathan* with a quotation from the Book of Job, translated as "There is no power on earth to be compared to him."

The social contract

In *Leviathan*, Hobbes contrasted the lawless state of nature with the political order of a civil society. In order to make the transition to such a society, he explained that there must be consent from all concerned—a social contract to give up "natural rights" and hand power to an authority that imposes and enforces laws. Although a social contract necessarily restricts the freedom of individuals, it protects them from what Hobbes saw as the evils of lawlessness. Hobbes argued that authority should ideally be given to a single person—a monarch or even a tyrant was preferable to a chaotic society.

Other philosophers accepted the idea of a social contract, but disagreed with Hobbes's preference for monarchy. John Locke, who had a less jaundiced opinion of human nature and a suspicion of authority, argued for a more egalitarian system in which power is given by the consent of the governed to protect natural freedoms, giving them civil rights, including the right to remove tyrannical or ineffective government.

The advent of a social contract establishing civil society meant an end to medieval feudalism.

Voltaire and
the *encyclopédistes*

Political philosophy in the Age of Reason found a distinctive voice in 18th-century France. Influenced by the social contract theory of Hobbes and especially Locke, some French thinkers argued for more representative government to replace the existing rule of monarch and aristocracy. Foremost among them were the compilers of the massive *Encyclopédie*, Denis Diderot and Jean le Rond d'Alembert, who believed that education would enable people to participate in politics, instead of simply accepting conventional authorities. They were also influenced by the campaign of Voltaire (see page 184) for separation of Church and state, freedom of speech and religion, and a generally more tolerant society. Voltaire himself was a deist, believing that reason and observation confirmed the existence of God, but had little time for the established Church; Diderot and d'Alembert became outspoken atheist materialists, challenging any religious authority or divine right to rule. Their criticism of government fell just short of demand for a republic, but was in tune with a growing mood of the time.

ENCYCLOPÉDIE,

OU

DICTIONNAIRE RAISONNÉ

DES SCIENCES,

DES ARTS ET DES MÉTIERS,

PAR UNE SOCIÉTÉ DE GENS DE LETTRES.

Mis en ordre & publié par M. *DIDEROT*, de l'Académie Royale des Sciences & des Belles-Lettres de Prusse ; & quant à la PARTIE MATHÉMATIQUE, par M. *D'ALEMBERT*, de l'Académie Royale des Sciences de Paris, de celle de Prusse, & de la Société Royale de Londres.

Tantùm series juncturaque pollet,
Tantùm de medio sumptis accedit honoris! HORAT.

TOME PREMIER.

A PARIS,

Chez
{
BRIASSON, *rue Saint Jacques, à la Science.*
DAVID l'aîné, *rue Saint Jacques, à la Plume d'or.*
LE BRETON, Imprimeur ordinaire du Roy, *rue de la Harpe.*
DURAND, *rue Saint Jacques, à Saint Landry, & au Griffon.*
}

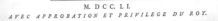

M. DCC. LI.

Jean-Jacques Rousseau

A new interpretation of the social contract was put forward by French philosopher Jean-Jacques Rousseau. He turned Hobbes's ideas (see page 176) on their head, arguing that humans are fundamentally good when given the freedom of a "state of nature," but this goodness is corrupted by modern culture: civil societies are formed to protect private property, not rights and freedoms, and their restrictive and unjust laws foster inequality. Rousseau's alternative was direct rule by the people, with legislation decided by the *volonté générale*, the general will: laws created by the people would encapsulate, rather than restrict, individual freedoms. He did, however, introduce a note of caution, saying that the people would need to be educated in order to know what their will really was.

Rousseau's rather idyllic ideas were later taken up by the Romantic movement (see page 268), but before then his famous declaration that "Man was born free yet everywhere he is in chains" was adopted as a rallying cry of the French Revolution.

Native American societies, which were not based on ideas of private property and land ownership, were closer to Rousseau's vision than European society.

Freedom

The political philosophy that developed from ideas of the social contract made frequent reference to the idea of freedom, but interpretations of this concept differed. Hobbes, for example, saw the unlimited freedom of a state of nature as an evil, and the surrender of freedom as necessary to civilized society. Locke, on the other hand, saw society as protecting the freedom of natural rights. Voltaire and the *encyclopédistes* believed in freedom from authoritarian rule, while Rousseau advocated freedom from society and convention, and Karl Marx later argued for freedom of the working class from exploitation (see page 284). While the French and American revolutions had "Liberty" as their watchword, 19th-century British liberalism centered on John Stuart Mill's principle of freedom to do as we please, provided that does not interfere with others' freedom to do likewise. Like the notions of justice and virtue explored by Greek philosophers, freedom is difficult to define and a thorough examination of the concept only came with the 20th-century work of Isaiah Berlin (see page 254).

The signing of the US Declaration of Independence was symbolic of a widespread desire for freedom in the 18th century.

Revolution: replacing old monarchies

Political change in Europe gathered pace in the 17th century, as the power of monarchy and aristocracy was challenged. Renaissance humanism had brought into question any divine right to rule, and in many places the classical idea of a democratic republic had been revived. Naturally, such ideas met with resistance, so the old orders were often removed by force. The first revolution of the Enlightenment was in England, when the monarchy was overthrown and power transferred to Parliament. This shift in political power prompted Hobbes and Locke to develop the theory of the social contract, and their political philosophy inspired philosophers and political thinkers elsewhere. In France, Voltaire, Diderot, and especially Rousseau seized upon the idea of the social contract to explain the necessity of change, while in America, Englishman Thomas Paine translated philosophy into political activism. The revolutions in America and France had similar political ideals embodied in the mottoes "Life, liberty, and the pursuit of happiness" and "*Liberté, égalité, fraternité,*" both inspired by Enlightenment philosophy.

Rationalism

Often known as the Age of Reason or Enlightenment, the 17th and 18th centuries were characterized by advances in knowledge through scientific reasoning, rather than faith or acceptance of conventional wisdom. In much of Europe, this manifested itself in the philosophical approach known as rationalism. Science, and mathematics in particular, inspired philosophers such as René Descartes, who argued that our senses are unreliable, so we can understand the world through rational thought. This approach to epistemology, the way we acquire knowledge, echoed Plato's distrust of sensory perception (see page 72). Descartes's rigorous approach marked a turning point in the history of philosophy, integrating mathematical method into philosophical inquiry. Rationalism was enthusiastically adopted by Spinoza and Gottfried Leibniz (both, significantly, accomplished mathematicians) and became the predominant school of philosophical thought in mainland Europe. In Britain, however, an opposing school of thought, empiricism, emerged from the same roots (see page 212).

The pure reasoning of mathematics was a significant influence on the emergence of 17th-century rationalism.

Descartes:
"Cogito, ergo sum"

René Descartes set out to approach the questions of metaphysics and epistemology in the same way as he would treat a mathematical proof. His method was to eliminate all the things there could be any doubt about, and try to establish certainties to work from—incontrovertible truths analogous to mathematical axioms.

He took the view of an extreme skeptic, arguing that we can not be sure of the existence of anything in the world around us, as our senses are easily deceived—it is even possible that we are deceived to the extent that all of what we consider reality is in fact illusion. There would seem to be no grounds for any certain knowledge, but Descartes's great insight was that because he is doubting everything, he must exist in order to do the doubting. *"Cogito, ergo sum"* ("I am thinking, therefore I exist" carries the idea better than the usual translation "I think, therefore I am") became the so-called First Certainty, which he used as the foundation for all his philosophical inquiries.

Mind–body dualism

In establishing *"Cogito, ergo sum"* as a First Certainty to work from, Descartes implicitly identifies himself as a thinking being. The "I" of "I think, therefore I am" is the part that thinks, distinct from the physical senses that can be deceived. From this, he inferred that the mind, the "thinking thing," is not only separate from the body, but is of a fundamentally different substance. This belief, so-called mind–body dualism, was not new—many classical philosophers believed in the existence of a "psyche" independent of the body, and most religions also believed in a realm inhabited by immortal souls—but Descartes was the first to present the case in a systematic way.

The distinctions made in this "substantive dualism," that our bodies are made of a physical, material substance and our minds of a mental, immaterial substance, extended to the outside world. Humans, because they are capable of reasoning, have minds as well as physical bodies. Things that cannot reason do not have minds and so only exist as material objects.

Descartes believed the senses carried information to the brain, where it was passed to an immaterial spirit or mind.

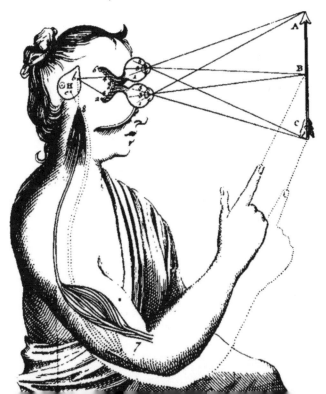

The ghost in the machine

With his idea of mind–body dualism, Descartes set the agenda for modern thinking in metaphysics. Not all philosophers agreed with him, however; some argued that everything that exists has a physical substance, others that all reality is fundamentally mental and immaterial. But in 1949, Gilbert Ryle challenged the distinction between mental and physical substances in *The Concept of Mind*. It is wrong, he said, to consider the mind as a place where thoughts, knowledge, and sensations exist in the same way as our physical senses reside in the body. Ryle dismissed the notion of an immaterial mental substance separate from a physical one as "the ghost in the machine," the result of a "category mistake." The error Cartesian dualism makes, he said, is to consider mind and body, or mental reality and physical reality, as if they belonged to the same logical category, and then describe them as polar opposites. This category mistake is the same as considering, for example, "the electorate" as some sort of ghostly entity separate from the people who vote in elections.

A classic category mistake would be a visitor to Oxford who sees its individual colleges, but then asks "Where is the University?"

The deceiving demon

To arrive at his famous *"Cogito, ergo sum,"* Descartes devised a thought experiment to narrow down the things we can be certain of. Suppose, he suggested, that there is an evil and powerful demon deceiving me about everything I think I know. Every belief I have is then thrown into doubt, as it could be the demon making me believe it. The only belief left to me that I can be certain of is my own existence, since the demon could not be deceiving me if I did not exist. This thought experiment is similar to the idea of the "flying man" (see page 158), deprived of information from all his physical senses, which led Avicenna to similar dualist conclusions. There are several modern versions of the "deceiving demon" concept, most famously the scenario that an evil scientist keeps my brain in a vat of nutrients and electrically stimulates it so that I experience physical sensations that give me an illusory sense of reality. More recently, this has been elaborated (notably in the movie *The Matrix*) to the suggestion that the world as we know it is a virtual one, a computer simulation we have been wired into.

Animals as automata

Advances in science and engineering during the 17th and 18th centuries fostered a mechanistic view of the physical world. Objects and their actions were explained in the same terms as machines, subject to the laws of physics. The difference between the physical and the mental in Descartes's dualism was stark, putting human thought and consciousness outside the physical realm. This was based on the idea that humans are capable of rational thought—but what of animals?

It was generally believed that animals were incapable of reasoning, so would not have minds to exist as immaterial mental substance in the same way as human minds. In the Cartesian view, animals are simply a part of the physical world, subject to physical laws, and behave in the same way as machines: it is a mistake to interpret their actions as evidence of consciousness or mental activity. This idea was reinforced at the time by ingenious automata that exhibited similar behavior to animals, but patently had no mind.

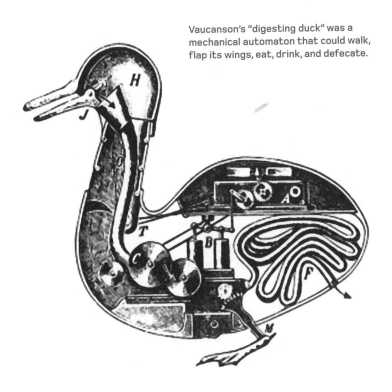

Vaucanson's "digesting duck" was a mechanical automaton that could walk, flap its wings, eat, drink, and defecate.

Other people's minds and consciousness

With his "*Cogito, ergo sum*," Descartes proved his own existence: he showed that the "I" of "I think" and "I am" exists as a thinking thing, a mind. But there is a problem with this sort of introspective reasoning. I know that I exist, and so have consciousness, but that does not prove that anybody else has; it would be wrong to assume on the evidence of a single example that this is a general rule. Common sense may persuade me that all human beings (and maybe even animals, see page 216) have the same sort of minds because they appear to me to exhibit consciousness, but that doesn't give me sufficient grounds for *believing* that they have. It may be that there are some people—philosophers call them "zombies" —who show all the outward signs of consciousness, such as wincing with pain, laughter, and so on, but actually have no consciousness. Perhaps everyone else is a zombie—I can never be sure. And even if they do have minds, I cannot know that the mental experiences of others are the same as mine; what I see as "red," for example, another person might see as my "green."

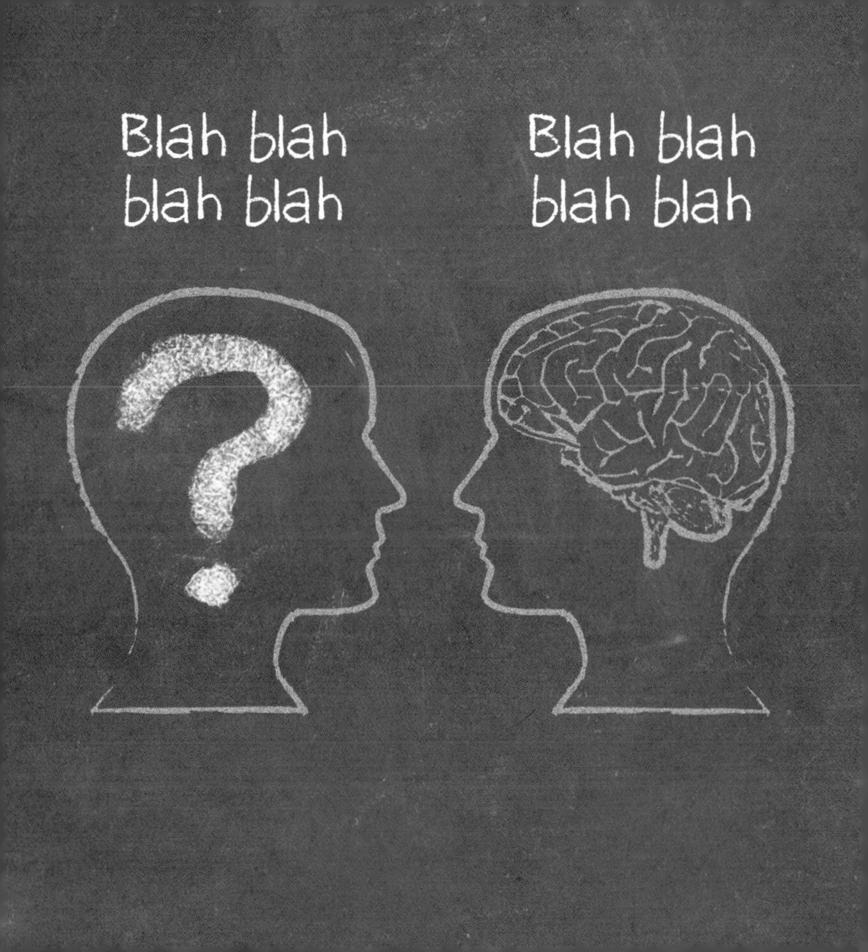
Blah blah
blah blah
Blah blah
blah blah

Identity

A carpenter has a favorite hammer that he has used for 50 years, with only two new heads and three new handles. Obviously, it is not the same hammer he started out with—or is it? This is a variation of the old tale of the Ship of Theseus, which underwent repairs throughout its lifetime until nothing original remained, yet still retained its identity.

Human beings go through a similar process of "running repairs," gradually replacing the cells of our bodies so that our physical makeup is completely different after a few years, yet we feel we are still the same person. It seems then that it is our minds, the immaterial substance that Cartesian dualism proposes, that determine our identities—or at least our knowledge, experience, and memory. Suppose, however, that it was possible to make a clone of yourself and transfer your thoughts and memories into its brain; to the outside world it would be indistinguishable from you, and would have every attribute of your identity, but intuitively we know that it is not *actually* you.

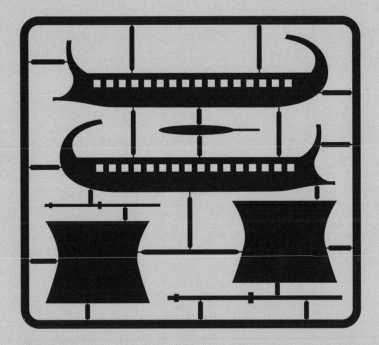

Does the Ship of Theseus have an identity independent of its component parts?

The mind-body problem

Critics of mind–body dualism pointed to a flaw in Descartes's theory. He maintained that mind and matter are essentially different: physical substance is material and incapable of thought, while mental substance is immaterial and does not exist in space. But we know from experience that the two interact: mental events bring about physical ones, and vice versa. There must be a connection between the two worlds—but where is it, and what is the nature of their interaction?

Descartes suggested it must happen somewhere in the brain, but this does not resolve the problem, as the brain is a physical object, separate from the immaterial mind in dualist theory. Others suggested that God forms the connection. For many philosophers, however, the mind-body problem led to a rejection of dualism in favor of some form of monism: that everything is either fundamentally physical (physicalism, or materialism), or immaterial (idealism). Spinoza proposed a theory incorporating aspects of both dualism and monism (see page 206).

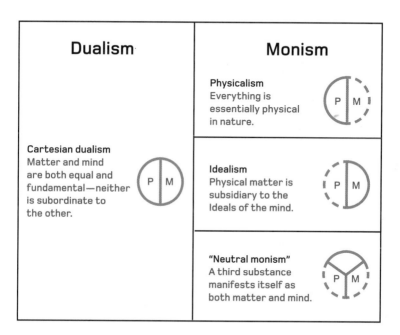

Dualism

Cartesian dualism
Matter and mind are both equal and fundamental—neither is subordinate to the other.

Monism

Physicalism
Everything is essentially physical in nature.

Idealism
Physical matter is subsidiary to the Ideals of the mind.

"Neutral monism"
A third substance manifests itself as both matter and mind.

Spinoza:
substance and attributes

The Dutch philosopher Benedict Spinoza was a lens-maker by trade, with a comprehensive knowledge of not only optics, but also physics, astronomy, and mathematics. As a philosopher, he was attracted to Descartes's rationalist epistemology, which fitted well with his own scientific thinking, but he did not agree with Descartes's mind–body dualism. Although he recognized that our rational thoughts are different from our physical senses, he could not accept that mind and body are separate, as they obviously interact, nor that there are two distinct mental and physical substances. Instead, in his book *Ethics*, he proposed a form of monism. Everything that exists consists of this one substance but, Spinoza believed, also has both physical and mental attributes: the single substance is neither exclusively physical nor mental, but exhibits aspects of both. Spinoza's "neutral monism" or "property dualism" provided a solution to the problem of interaction between separate material and immaterial substances posed by Descartes's substantive dualism (see page 192).

Spinoza:
God and nature

Spinoza was a profoundly religious man and was concerned that little place was given to God in the increasingly mechanistic interpretation of the universe, other than as its creator. He believed that God is not separate from the world, any more than the mental and physical are separate, and that God is infinite and all-pervasive, so there cannot be anything that God is not—he is not outside the world, nor is he in it, but he *is* the world. God, for Spinoza, is the one substance that constitutes the world and has both physical and mental properties, so our religious, philosophical, and scientific conceptions of it are simply different aspects of the same reality. Everything that exists is composed of the same substance, so the universe, or nature, and God are the same thing. This belief that God and nature are identical—pantheism—became influential in the Romantic movement (see page 268), but Spinoza's beliefs were seen at the time as tantamount to atheism: he was excommunicated from the synagogue and his *Tractatus Theologico-Politicus* was banned by the Church.

TRACTATUS

THEOLOGICO-

POLITICUS

Continens

Diſſertationes aliquot,

Quibus oſtenditur Libertatem Philoſophandi non tantum
ſalva Pietate, & Reipublicæ Pace poſſe concedi: ſed
eandem niſi cum Pace Reipublicæ, ipſaque
Pietate tolli non poſſe.

Auctore Benedicto de Spinoza.

Johann: Epiſt: I. Cap: IV. verſ: XIII.

*Per hoc cognoſcimus quod in Deo manemus, & Deus manet
in nobis, quod de Spiritu ſuo dedit nobis.*

HAMBURGI,
Apud *Henricum Künrath.* cɪɔ ɪɔ cɪxx.

"Two kinds of truths"

Like Descartes, Gottfried Leibniz contributed as much to mathematics as philosophy. His stance was essentially rationalist, but although he believed that knowledge should be accessible by reasoning, he recognized that rational faculties are imperfect and some knowledge must come from the external world. Leibniz identified "two kinds of truths: truths of reasoning and truths of fact." We can establish the truth of a statement such as "all bachelors are unmarried" by analysing its terms without reference to facts; but to explore the truth of "bachelors live longer than married men" we would need to look to the facts of the matter. The difference between these two types of statement, referred to by later philosophers as analytic and synthetic respectively, becomes particularly clear if we deny them: a truth of reasoning (a "necessary" truth), such as 2 + 2 = 4, is impossible to deny without logical contradiction, whereas denial of a truth of fact (a "contingent" truth), such as "water boils at 212°F," simply creates another synthetic statement, not a logical impossibility.

NECESSARY TRUTH:

All squares have
four sides.

CONTINGENT TRUTH:

All cows have
four legs.

Empiricism

Advances in science during the Age of Reason had a very different influence on British philosophy to that of mainland Europe. Reacting against the rationalism of Descartes, Spinoza, and Leibniz, British philosophers dismissed the idea that reason is our only reliable source of knowledge and developed the opposing movement known as empiricism. While not denying that reasoning is important to *assessing* information, the empiricists believed that the source of that information is the outside world, accessed through our senses. British empiricists were particularly influenced by Francis Bacon's scientific methodology of observation, analysis, and experiment (see page 174), which contrasted with the mathematically inspired reasoning of the continental rationalists. In the 17th century, Thomas Hobbes laid the foundations of modern empiricism with his materialist and mechanistic views— although its roots could be traced back to Aristotle, it was now reinforced by scientific advances and soon became established as the dominant philosophy of the English-speaking world.

British empiricist philosophy was influenced by the method of observation and experiment of the natural sciences, as opposed to the pure reasoning of mathematics that inspired continental rationalism.

Thomas Hobbes:
man as machine

Thomas Hobbes took an active interest in the scientific discoveries of the 17th century. He corresponded regularly with mathematicians including Descartes, but came to very different conclusions. Prompted by the debate over Cartesian mind–body dualism, he declared himself an outright materialist, dismissing the concept of "immaterial substance" as a contradiction in terms (a brave declaration at a time when belief in God was still virtually compulsory). Everything in the universe is physical or material, and nothing exists outside it.

Influenced by the astronomy of Copernicus and Galileo, Hobbes took a mechanistic view of the workings of the universe, arguing that even humans could be considered as machines subject to physical laws. He was especially intrigued by Galileo's theories of motion and impetus, which he believed explained not only the behavior of our bodies, but also our mental activity. Our minds, he argued, are physical "machines," and our psychology is ruled by the same physical laws as everything else in the universe.

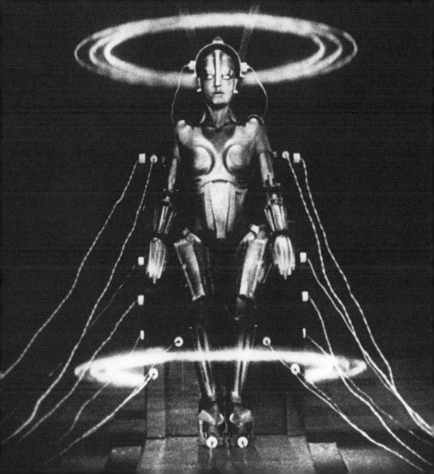

Animal rights

Hobbes's materialist view of man as machine was to have much later implications in the field of computers and artificial intelligence, but also raised questions about the minds of other living things. Descartes believed that only humans had conscious minds, and regarded animals as automata (see page 198). But if Hobbes was right, and despite being mere machines, we are still capable of reasoning and consciousness, perhaps the same is true of animals (unless they are "zombies" —see page 200). The argument for animals having similar minds to our own became even stronger with Darwin's theory of evolution in the 19th century and its implication that humans are simply another species of animal. If animals have similar "minds" to humans, then perhaps they can feel pain, fear, and all the other things that we do. Accepting this raises moral, and even political questions: should our actions toward animals be as morally correct as they are toward other humans? Is it right for us to restrict their liberty, or worse, take their lives? In short, should animals have the same rights as humans?

Locke and the limits of the knowable

While Hobbes prepared the ground for British empiricism, it was John Locke who first laid out its arguments. In his *Essay Concerning Human Understanding* (1689), Locke set out to discover the limits of what we can know. We can only apprehend "ideas" (by which he meant sensations, feelings, and so on, as well as intellectual ideas) in our own consciousness. But innate ideas, he reasoned, are an impossibility, as they cannot exist before there is a mechanism to think them, so our senses are the only source of information of external reality. That being the case, our knowledge depends on our sensory experience of the world; it is experience that determines the limits of what humans can know, no matter what actually exists externally. Locke believed that at birth we have faculties of sensory perception and a capacity for rational thought, but our minds are otherwise a *tabula rasa* or blank slate, with no innate ideas of the world. As well as providing a counterargument to Descartes's rationalism, this concept also influenced Locke's political philosophy (see page 178).

To be is to be perceived

Anglo-Irish philosopher George Berkeley took the arguments put forward by Locke to extremes, proposing a theory of "immaterialism"—that material substance does not exist. Locke established that all we can directly apprehend is the content of our own consciousness; Berkeley argued this means we can only have *indirect* sensory experience of things. And where Locke described objective, measurable "primary qualities" of things we experience, and subjective "secondary qualities," Berkeley pointed out that we do not actually experience things at all, *only* their qualities. Because we perceive ideas, not things in themselves, we have no grounds for believing anything exists other than ideas and the minds that perceive them: things only exist if they either perceive or are perceived. Material substance, therefore, does not exist, and Berkeley, a Christian bishop, explained reality as existing in the mind of God. The classic example of his idea that "to be is to be perceived" is a tree falling in a forest: does it make a sound if there is nobody there to hear it?

Hume and causality

Probably the most important of the empiricists was David Hume. He agreed with Locke's argument that we acquire knowledge only through experience, but realized that consistent application of this principle means we cannot know anything with certainty. The major drawback of empirical knowledge, he pointed out, is that just because we see something happen after something else doesn't prove there is a cause-and-effect relationship. But this notion that one thing causes another is fundamental to any attempt to understand the world; causal relationships help us to see a structure to the universe rather than just a collection of separate, unrelated events. Hume argued that apparent causal relationships are simply "constant conjunctions" of events. We assume that a billiard ball will move when struck by another, because in our experience this has always happened. But a clock set slightly slow will consistently chime a few minutes after one that is correct, yet we do not infer a causal relationship. Intuitively, we know the cases are different, but what are our grounds for thinking that?

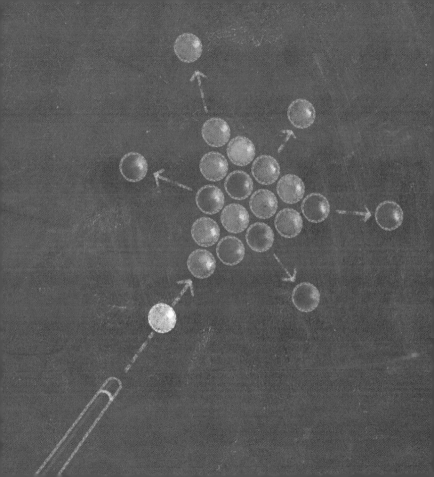

Hume's fork

The rationalist Leibniz had famously made the distinction between "two kinds of truths" (see page 210), those of reasoning and those of fact. Hume agreed, classifying statements as either "relations of ideas" or "matters of fact," akin to two different directions after a fork in the road. But Hume used the idea in a very different way from Leibniz. Truths of the first kind, analytic statements about ideas, are certain but depend on the definition of the terms they use, while truths of the second kind, synthetic statements of fact, refer to actual things in the world that we cannot be certain about. For example, the analytic statement "a square has four sides of equal length" can be proved true as a relation of ideas, but since such perfection does not exist in the world, it tells us nothing about the world and does not prove a matter of fact. Nothing, Hume concluded, can be both certain *and* tell us something about the world; we cannot cross the fork from one road to the other and use a relation of ideas to prove a matter of fact.

The problem of induction

In casting doubt on the notion of causality and our certainty about our knowledge of the world (see pages 222 and 224), Hume challenged the basis of modern scientific methodology. He simply pointed out that just because something always *has* happened, we cannot be sure it always *will* happen: we cannot say that something *causes* it to happen. To deny, for example, that the Sun will rise tomorrow doesn't produce a contradictory relation of ideas and isn't an impossible matter of fact—so we have no rational grounds for believing it. This means that induction—deriving a general rule from a series of individual instances—is not logically valid, raising a huge problem for science, which uses induction to form theories and general laws based on empirical observations and repeatable experiments. This "problem of induction" worried philosophers until Karl Popper proposed a solution in the 20th century (see page 366). Hume addressed it in characteristically good-humored fashion, saying that we just have to deal in hopeful probabilities, not certainties, and should let custom be our guide.

Astronomical clocks such as this one in Prague show the positions of the heavenly bodies based on countless observations—but can we be sure their movements are predictable?

Common sense

A distinguishing feature of British empiricism was its appeal to common sense. This tradition of no-nonsense reasoning had its roots in William of Ockham's reduction of unnecessary propositions and abstractions and Francis Bacon's methodical examination of evidence for any hypothesis (see pages 148 and 174). Locke repeatedly referred to "the plain facts of the matter," and while Berkeley's "subjective idealism" was an exception to this rule, his ideas were subsequently refuted by the down-to-earth Hume. But Hume realized that logical reasoning often leads us to conclusions that are difficult to accept, and in those cases we must use our experience to weigh up the evidence and make judgments. He was also skeptical of all things supernatural: "miracles" that, by definition, violate the laws of nature derived from our experience of the world. Common sense (also part of our experience of the world) tells us that the likelihood that an event contradicting all our experience is miraculous is less than the probability that our senses have been deceived or that the account of it is false.

Miracles such as the feeding of the 5,000 apparently defy the laws of nature, but it is more likely our senses our being deceived or the story has been made up.

Reason is the
slave of passions

Hume effectively removed all grounds for relying on reason in dealing with the world around us. For our expectations of the future, he suggested that we let custom be our guide, advocating a "mitigated skepticism" that appeals to common sense. Still, he recognized that we generally make judgments and take decisions based on our emotional and instinctive drives, what he called "the passions," rather than our reason.

More often than not, he observed, our reason is overruled by our passions, and we only use rational thought to justify or satisfy them. Emotions such as love and hate, and drives such as hunger, libido, and self-preservation, are very powerful and persuasive, even in situations where reason tells us there are no rational grounds for our decision. Because, in Hume's phrase, reason is the slave of the passions, we sometimes make the wrong judgments—but on balance it is better to do something to satisfy our passions than to deny our essential urges because we have no rational justification for them.

Letting our hearts rule our heads sometimes has tragic consequences, such as the deaths of Shakespeare's Romeo and Juliet.

Is vs. ought

Hume's skepticism about the role of reason in our decision-making (see page 230) extended to his views on moral philosophy. He remarked that in the writings of most moral philosophers, there is a sudden shift from objective description to subjective prescription: the writer jumps from statements using "is" or "is not" to propositions using "ought" or "ought not." The change, in his opinion, needed explanation, and given his view that reason alone did not give grounds for certainty, deriving an "ought" from an "is" was not a justifiable basis for forming moral judgments. The 20th-century British philosopher A.J. Ayer agreed with Hume, arguing that this "naturalistic fallacy" does no more than show how the writer feels about a statement. Ayer's theory of emotivism, or the "boo-hurrah theory," shows that moral propositions may look like statements of objective fact, but are actually subjective. When someone says "Murder is wrong," it is really an emotional appeal for the response "Murder? Boo!," while "Philanthropy is good" really means "Let's hear it for philanthropy! Hurrah!."

Knowledge: justified true belief?

The difference between the rationalist and empiricist schools rested primarily on the way in which they believed we acquire knowledge—but what exactly *is* knowledge? The definition established by the classical Greeks is that it is "justified true belief"—something becomes knowledge when three conditions are met: I believe it, it is factually true, and I have verifiable justification for believing it. In the 1960s, however, Edmund Gettier showed that these conditions are not enough. Suppose a farmer is worried his cow is missing. A friend assures him that he has seen the cow in the field, so the farmer goes to check and sees the black-and-white shape of his cow. The friend also checks, but finds the cow hidden in some trees and a large piece of black-and-white paper in the field, so he realizes the farmer mistook the paper for the cow. The farmer *believes* the cow was in the field, it is *factually true* that it is, and he is *justified* in the belief by the testimony of his friend—but in this case, is it right to say that he *knows* that it is?

Positivism

While empiricism developed primarily in Britain to rival continental rationalism, a small but influential movement based on the principles of scientific method also emerged in France. The central idea of this movement, positivism, was that the only valid knowledge is that which can be positively verified, so truth can only be found in scientific knowledge.

The leading figure of the positivists was Auguste Comte, who felt that metaphysical speculation should no longer play a part in philosophy, and should be replaced by scientific inquiry. Breaking with the continental tradition of rationalism, he advocated the empirical process of observation, theory formation, and verification to establish knowledge of the world. Positivism was a symptom of the slowly widening division between science and philosophy, but Comte is also considered a pioneer in the modern philosophy of science (see page 360), the branch of philosophy that examines the foundations and methods of science, and its wider implications.

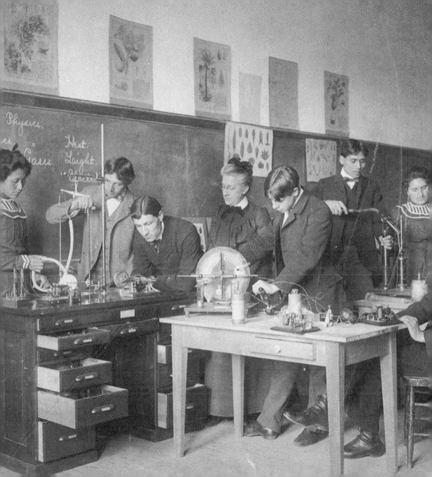

Sociological positivism

Positivism (see page 236) proposed that only scientifically verifiable knowledge could be considered valid. This, according to Auguste Comte, not only applied to the natural sciences, but was also a valid principle in considering human social behavior. Comte argued that society operates according to discoverable laws, in the same way that the physical world is subject to physical laws, and we cannot gain knowledge of society from subjective introspection or intuition, but only through objective scientific study. This idea was the basis of the modern discipline of sociology, and influenced the sociologist Emile Durkheim in the late 19th century to give the subject an even more scientific footing through practical research. Comte was also influential in the foundation of other social sciences, including anthropology, economics, and political science. And although Karl Marx rejected Comte's sociological positivism as such, he shared the view that metaphysical philosophizing was irrelevant to the modern world and that theories in the social sciences should be justified using scientific methods.

On the Origin of Species

The cultural influence of science reached a climax in the mid-19th century with the 1859 publication of Darwin's *On the Origin of Species*. Although it was a scientific rather than a philosophical work, his theory of evolution by natural selection put many aspects of philosophy in a new perspective. In the same way as Copernicus's proposal of a heliocentric universe challenged religious authority and became symbolic of emergent Renaissance humanism, Darwin's explanation of evolution presented humans as just another animal—part of the natural world rather than separate from it. In his later *Descent of Man*, he applied the principles of evolutionary theory specifically to humans, explicitly stating for the first time that we have evolved from animals, and so challenging previous notions of man as superior to other animals because of his ability to reason. But perhaps most important in terms of its effect on philosophy was the implicit idea that humans are not the pinnacle of God's creation, but merely a stage in the evolution of the natural world.

Evolution, creationism, and intelligent design

Darwin's theory of natural selection further widened the gap between science and religion that had opened since the Renaissance. *On the Origin of Species* clearly contradicted the biblical account of creation and reignited the faith versus reason debate. On one side were creationists who believed in the literal truth of the Bible, on the the other, the supporters of Darwin. But in the middle an argument for the existence of God from intelligent design had persisted (see page 122), which was now effectively refuted by Darwin's theory: the diversity of life, including humans, is the result of organisms adapting to circumstances, and the apparent "cleverness" of living things is a matter of suitability to an environment, not design.

Darwin had been raised as a Christian, but became increasingly agnostic as he developed his theory, although he continued to believe in the existence of a God. Like Isaac Newton, he believed that God created the universe and its governing laws such as natural selection, but then had no further cause to intervene.

1. Geospiza magnirostris.
2. Geospiza fortis.
3. Geospiza parvula.
4. Certhidea olivasea.

By observing features such as the various shapes of finches' beaks, Darwin concluded that the diversity of species was the result of evolution, not an immutable, divine design.

British liberalism

At the end of the 18th century, rapidly industrializing nations in Europe and America sought to establish democratic institutions. Following the revolutions in America and France, constitutions were drawn up to ensure social justice and individual freedoms. Britain's own revolution, a century before, had established a constitutional monarchy, and British political philosophers were arguably in a better position to theorize about the organization of democratic society and the balance between authority and liberty. While elsewhere in Europe the emphasis on metaphysics remained, British thinkers focused on moral and political philosophy, building on the legacy of social contract theory, and Hume's practical empiricism (see pages 178 and 222). A tradition of liberalism (in the sense of *laissez-faire*, rather than left-wing) emerged in the conservative liberalism of Edmund Burke and economic liberalism of Adam Smith. Jeremy Bentham, meanwhile, proposed a more radical moral and political philosophy that was to influence the most prominent 19th-century British philosopher, John Stuart Mill.

Political economy

As well as his influential work on the problem of empirical knowledge (see page 222), David Hume took an interest in political philosophy, and in particular questions of trade in goods and services. He was one of a circle of intellectuals based in Edinburgh alongside Adam Smith, who shared many of Hume's ideas and developed them into a full-blown theory of political economy in *The Wealth of Nations* (1776). Smith's work marked a shift away from moral philosophy toward the more scientific approach of modern economics. He explained that humans act out of self-interest, but in civil societies have to cooperate; we require goods and services, so we make bargains in order to exchange these for mutual benefit. Led by the "invisible hand" of the market, the self-interest of individual traders also works to the benefit of society as a whole. Smith therefore advocated economic liberalism—that there should be minimal government interference in the working of a free market to allow these benefits to provide us with the freedom to enjoy our "natural liberty."

Adam Smith stressed the importance of the marketplace as an exchange of goods and services for mutual benefit.

Conservatism

In striking a balance between liberty and authority, "classical liberalism," as it came to be known, recommended that government should interfere as little as possible with the freedoms of its citizens. But among liberal thinkers, some held conservative views about who should rule, and how society should change. British parliamentarian Edmund Burke, for example, famously supported American independence and argued for relaxation of political and economic pressure on the colonies, but as a conservative was opposed to the revolution in France. Burke believed that societies develop gradually into complex systems built on generations of accumulated wisdom —it is wrong to think that the theories of a single thinker or small group could suddenly replace the structure of a society that had evolved organically. He also thought that there should be a ruling class to safeguard the material and cultural assets of society, and that the aristocracy, born and brought up in a tradition of ruling with the experience of generations before them, were the best qualified for this role.

English country houses such as Chatsworth are often seen as bastions of the conservative ruling class ideal.

Bentham and utilitarianism

At the end of the 18th century, a movement of "freethinkers" in Britain developed that were influenced as much by prerevolutionary French political philosophy as they were by British empiricism. Among them was Jeremy Bentham, who proposed a utilitarian system of moral philosophy, in which an action is judged by its usefulness in bringing about beneficial consequences: a morally good action maximizes pleasure and minimizes pain. In quasi-scientific fashion, Bentham devised a "calculus of felicity" in which "the greatest happiness of the greatest number ... is the measure of right and wrong." He applied the same principle to politics, emphasizing that in his calculus "everybody is to count for one, and nobody for more than one." On this basis, many prevailing laws and conventions were seen as unnecessarily authoritarian, especially those concerning personal morality, while laws allowing, for example, exploitation of workers were unduly lax. Bentham's idea's inspired many 19th-century social reforms, and later influenced the foundation of a British socialist movement.

On Liberty

In Bentham's utilitarianism, the rightness of actions is judged by their consequences, how much pleasure or pain they cause. This was in distinct contrast to Immanuel Kant's system of moral philosophy based on the motives of an action and a moral "categorical imperative," which influenced European ideas of morality (see page 264). The British liberal, *laissez-faire* approach to government and economics also distinguished it from more ideological political philosophies elsewhere. The morality of motives, such as the self-interest pointed out by Adam Smith (see page 246), is less important than the beneficial results for society. John Stuart Mill, whose father was a friend of Bentham, was a great advocate of utilitarian moral principles, but also of liberal political ideals of personal freedom. In his book *On Liberty*, Mill offered a less rigid version of utilitarianism, shifting the emphasis to the liberty of the individual and introducing the "harm principle." In his opinion, people should be free to do as they like, so long as it does not harm anyone else or restrict their ability to do the same.

The British police force was established to protect the interests of the people rather than to impose authoritarian laws.

Two Concepts of Liberty

The concept of liberty as the freedom of individuals to go about their lives, so long as this harms no one else, was taken almost for granted until the mid-20th century. But in his *Two Concepts of Liberty* (1958), Isaiah Berlin explained that what we generally call liberty is *negative* freedom, freedom from external interference. What he called *positive* freedom, on the other hand, comes from within, from having the resources to achieve personal autonomy and realize one's own potential. While negative freedom is defined by our interaction with others, positive freedom is concerned with personal development, though it can be fostered by recognition and participation in a positive social context. Berlin believed both negative and positive freedoms are valuable, but that positive freedom carries dangers. People with personal positive freedom can become tyrannical, as happened to Robespierre in postrevolutionary France. The result is freedom only for the powerful—as Berlin puts it: "In a lake stocked with minnows and minnow-eating pike, freedom for the pike means death to the minnows."

The rights of women

The democracies that followed the revolutions in France and America were established on principles of liberty and equality. There was frequent reference to "natural rights," especially in the French *Declaration of the Rights of Man and of the Citizen* of 1789. However, the playwright Olympe de Gouges pointed out a glaring omission with her response, the *Declaration of the Rights of Woman and the Female Citizen*. In Britain, Mary Wollstonecraft similarly replied to Thomas Paine's *Rights of Man* with *A Vindication of the Rights of Woman*. A major step toward equal rights for women came with philosopher Harriet Taylor's friendship with and later marriage to John Stuart Mill. He saw her as an intellectual equal, and as a respected philosopher and Member of Parliament, was better able to promote her cause, writing *The Subjection of Women* based on her ideas. The first male philosopher since Plato and Epicurus to advocate sexual equality, he campaigned for women's rights, and in 1866 became the first MP to propose votes for women.

German idealism

While French and British philosophers dominated the Enlightenment period, from the 1780s philosophy began to flourish more in the German-speaking world. Immanuel Kant was the first of the great German philosophers, introducing ideas that became the starting point for a century of German philosophy. Bringing together the apparently opposing views of rationalism and empiricism, Kant proposed a metaphysics he called "transcendental idealism," which explained the world as we experience it through our senses at the same time as admitting the existence of a world we cannot apprehend, the world as it is in itself. His ideas inspired followers included Schelling, Fichte, Schopenhauer, and Hegel, each with his own interpretation of idealism. Idealism also provoked a reaction, as philosophers such as Feuerbach and Marx adapted some of Hegel's ideas to argue for a materialist view. This was also critical of religion and marked the beginnings of an increasingly skeptical, atheist philosophy culminating in Nietzsche's famous declaration that "God is dead."

From the late 18th century, German culture—
music, literature, art, and philsophy—dominated
the Western world for more than 100 years.

Reconciling rationalism and empiricism

Until late in his career, Immanuel Kant was a rationalist—he claimed that he was awoken from this "dogmatic slumber" by reading the works of Hume (see page 222), and was also influenced by scientific advances to admit the importance of empirically derived evidence. He set about reconciling the two apparently opposing theories of rationalism and empiricism in his 1781 magnum opus, the *Critique of Pure Reason*. Kant argued that we have what he called a "sensibility," enabling us to recognize objects in space and time, but also an "understanding" of concepts such as space, time, and substance. He called these concepts "categories" of understanding (including substance, quantity, quality, relation, and modality), and reasoned that, since we must have knowledge of these concepts in order to understand the things we recognize empirically, they must be *a priori*, or innate. So, while we get to know some things about the world empirically, through our bodily senses, prior to that experience we innately understand the parameters, the "categories," that define them.

Phenomenon and noumenon

In the *Critique of Pure Reason*, Kant wanted to find the limits of what we can apprehend and subject to reasoning. We apprehend things only through bodily experience, but there may be things that we cannot experience, but which nevertheless exist in reality. There are, Kant explains, two worlds: the world as we experience it through our senses, and the world as it is in itself. What our senses tell us is not complete—what we see, hear, and touch gives us *information* about a thing, but that is not the thing itself. Kant made the distinction between the *noumenon*, the thing-in-itself, and the *phenomenon*, the thing as we experience it. The noumenal world is transcendental—it exists beyond our experience and apprehension. But we perceive the phenomenal world through our senses and the categories of understanding, so it is both empirically real *and* transcendentally ideal. Kant called his theory "transcendental idealism." So, while science can discover things about the phenomenal world, the nature of reality independent of experience will always be beyond our understanding.

The categorical imperative

Kant developed his ideas of "transcendental idealism" into a comprehensive system of philosophy that included epistemology, metaphysics, and ethics. The cornerstone of his moral philosophy was a belief that as rational creatures, we have innate concepts of good and bad, and the free will to make moral choices. But he broke with tradition and argued that morality should be judged on intentions or motives, not consequences. If there is a valid reason that something is right or wrong, he believed, then it must be *universally* valid. Morality is based on reason, just as science is, and moral laws, like the laws of physics, can have no exceptions. Kant famously expressed this categorical imperative as "Act only according to maxims which you can will also to be universal laws," later adding the notion that it is always wrong to treat others as simply a means to an end. The idea of universal moral laws may be attractive, but it is as hard to justify as purely consequentialist ethics. For example, if we believe lying is always wrong, then is it morally bad to lie to protect the runaway slave we are hiding?

Morality is reality

Kant's version of idealism was taken a step further in the philosophy of Johann Gottlieb Fichte. Although an admirer of Kant, Fichte dismissed the concept of the *noumenon*, or thing-in-itself, and proposed a system of absolute idealism, in which external reality is the creation of the knowing mind.

Hume and Kant had shown that scientific laws could not be derived from empirical observations (see page 262), but Fichte believed that the converse is possible. He believed that the laws of physics proposed by Newton, for example, were true, and argued that we have an innate idea of the structure of the universe, from which we deduce empirical reality. The knowing subject, what he calls the "I," is the cause of external reality, the "not-I." In this view, the self is not a passive observer but is active and free to make choices, implying that our existence is essentially moral. From this, Fichte argued that reality, as a creation of that moral self, must also be fundamentally moral in character.

"What sort of philosophy one chooses depends on what sort of person one is."
—Johann Gottlieb Fichte

Idealism and nature

The period of German idealism coincided with the growth of the Romantic movement in the arts. With its emphasis on emotion and fascination with nature, Romanticism developed as a reaction to scientific rationalization and industrialization, but was also influenced by Rousseau's view of a state of nature and Spinoza's pantheism (see pages 182 and 208).

Among the circle of German Romantic artists, writers, and intellectuals was Friedrich Schelling, whose philosophy of nature chimed with their ideals. Schelling reacted against Fichte's ideas, arguing that a knowing subject cannot exist without an object, and vice versa. Reality is not a creation of the "I"—there is no difference between subjective experience and objective external reality. So life is not separate from matter, and nature is a living thing, a continually developing process characterized by its creativity. For Schelling, human creativity represents the highpoint of nature's development toward self-awareness.

German Romantic artists such as Caspar David Friedrich explored the relationship between man and nature.

The World as Will and Representation

Arthur Schopenhauer was a great admirer of Kant and avidly absorbed his idea of phenomenon and noumenon. In his book *The World as Will and Representation* (1818) he took the idea a step further, proposing that there are not two separate worlds, but one world with two different aspects. What Kant described as the noumenal world cannot consist of things-in-themselves, Schopenhauer argued, as in order to be different from one another they would have to exist in different places in time or space—and time and space are a part of the phenomenal world. What's more, noumena cannot cause phenomena, as causality also only exists in the phenomenal world; so acts of will (which are noumenal) cannot cause things like bodily movement. He concluded that Will and movement are therefore one and the same thing. The phenomenal and noumenal are not separate worlds but the same, experienced in two different ways: Will from within, and Representation, from outside. We can experience our own Will, but only the Representation, not the inner Will, of other things.

Man can do what he wills, but he cannot WILL what he wills.

(A. Schopenhauer)

The Universal Will

According to Schopenhauer, the world is experienced from outside as Representation, and from within as Will. The whole of what Kant had called the noumenal world, Schopenhauer said was characterized by Will. And because time and space do not exist in the noumenal realm, there can be no differentiation; the Will must be universal, indivisible, and timeless, and therefore includes the Will present in every individual thing, including ourselves. Every individual's Will is part of the one Universal Will, which he saw as without consciousness or intelligence, impersonal, and aimless. It is like a form of energy, controlling the world of Representation, including our basic urges and instincts. Schopenhauer believed that attempts to satisfy such desires are doomed to disappointment and frustration. The only hope of salvation is to give up any illusion of separation from the Universal Will, and any hope of gratification, and accept that one day we will not exist. This is strikingly similar to Hindu and Buddhist beliefs, which Schopenhauer later studied enthusiastically.

19th-century opium dens epitomized the hopelessness
of seeking personal gratification.

Reality is a
historical process

Like Kant, Georg Hegel developed a "system" of philosophy, but while building on Kant's ideas, he corrected what he saw as fundamental errors in Kant's thinking. Hegel dismissed the notion of a thing-in-itself as a mere abstraction, and argued that what exists is whatever is manifested in consciousness. Being, for Hegel, is a single and comprehensive whole within which a thinking subject—consciousness—and its object—the external world—are identical. What he called the *Geist*, or Spirit, encompasses everything in this essentially nonmaterial reality, including our institutions and consciousness. Hegel also rejected the idea that Kant's "categories," our framework of experience, are distinct and unchanging. Instead, he believed that consciousness itself, and not just that which we are conscious of, is subject to change and part of a process of evolution. We see changes in the world as the progress of history, but more than that, these are examples of changes in the Spirit as a whole: reality itself is a dynamic, historical process.

Revolutions, especially the Haitian slave revolt in the 1790s, confirmed for Hegel the idea of a change in Spirit being a necessary part of social change.

Hegel's dialectic

Having described reality as a historical process (see page 274), Hegel then pursued the idea that not only is the Spirit that comprises reality constantly evolving, but also this process has an underlying structure. He explained this in terms of a dialectical progression: every notion, he maintained, contains within itself a contradictory notion, and the antagonism between the two opposing notions is resolved by the emergence of a new notion. The first notion he called the "thesis," its contradiction the "'antithesis," and the resulting new notion the "synthesis." Within a thesis such as the notion of a tyrannical regime, for example, the notion of freedom from tyranny is present as an antithesis. The resolution of these opposing notions, the synthesis, would be the notion of justice through the rule of law. The synthesis is richer in meaning than the thesis from which it is derived, implying not only a historical progression of events, but also a process that allows the Spirit (including our own thought and consciousness) to achieve a better, truer understanding of itself.

SYNTHESIS

Progress

THESIS   Tension   ANTITHESIS

Alienation and the *Zeitgeist*

Hegel believed that there is a single reality, and that this is essentially not material, but what he called *Geist*, or Spirit. The phenomena we perceive, even our own thoughts and consciousness, are simply aspects of this one Spirit, which is continually evolving in time through a process of dialectic. As a result, each period of time has its own different Spirit, the *Zeitgeist* or Spirit of the age, in which our way of thinking and consciousness is at a specific stage in its development.

We are all caught up in this *Zeitgeist*, living within its ideas and institutions, which we also play a part in creating. However, these often constrain us with codes of conduct that may be alien to the way we would like to live. Despite being part of the *Zeitgeist*, our own ideas can be out of tune with the world around us, and we feel a sense of "alienation" from the very social and political institutions we have created. This may even extend to our religious institutions, by projecting our ideals onto a God who is separate from our world.

Materialism and atheism

Although greatly influenced by Hegel, Ludwig Feuerbach developed a philosophy that was almost his polar opposite. Where Hegel was an idealist, believing reality was ultimately immaterial, Feuerbach was a materialist, denying the existence of any immaterial realm. And where Hegel had said that we project our ideals onto God, the "Absolute Spirit," Feuerbach went further and suggested that we have in fact created an imaginary being embodying these ideals and then called it "God." Theology, he said, is simply anthropology, and rather than looking to the divine for guidance, we should examine ourselves as the true source of the virtues we ascribe to it. Feuerbach's moral philosophy was firmly based on this idea of human rather than godly virtues. His ideas were later adopted by some right-wing political philosophers, but Feuerbach was a left-liberal and his influence was most clearly felt in the philosophy of political revolution. His atheistic materialism became the link between Hegel's notions of the dialectical process of historical change and the *Zeitgeist*, and the ideas of Karl Marx.

Dialectical materialism

As a student, Karl Marx became interested in the theories of Hegel, and especially the dialectic of historical progress. But, along with other left-wing "young Hegelians," he saw the dialectic as a political and social process. Marx was a materialist and an admirer of Feuerbach, but came to reject the contemporary German preoccupation with metaphysics, famously declaring "The philosophers have only interpreted the world, in various ways. The point, however, is to change it."

By adopting the framework of Hegel's dialectic and applying it to his own ideas, Marx analysed the historical process in terms of social and economic relations rather than Spirit. In this dialectical materialism, contradictions of thesis and antithesis were those of the struggle between classes. From the thesis of feudal lords and antithesis of serfs, for example, came the synthesis of city life. Marx believed that philosophy could not only analyse history as a series of class struggles, but also provide a vision for future progress to a classless society.

MARX'S ANALYSIS OF HISTORY

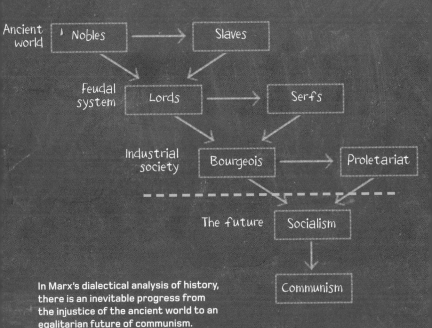

Ancient world → Nobles → Slaves

Feudal system → Lords → Serfs

Industrial society → Bourgeois → Proletariat

The future → Socialism → Communism

In Marx's dialectical analysis of history, there is an inevitable progress from the injustice of the ancient world to an egalitarian future of communism.

Das Kapital

Marx's political philosophy was based on a view of history as a series of class struggles. By the mid-19th century the antagonism was clearly between the working class "proletariat," and their capitalist employers. Capitalism had become the predominant economic system of the industrialized world, and as part of his analysis of the contemporary class struggle Marx wrote a comprehensive critique of it, *Das Kapital*. The owners of the means of production are motivated by profit, he argued, through accumulation of capital that is produced by their workforce. Marx saw this as a fundamentally exploitative relationship, in which the workers are forced to maintain a system that oppresses them, ultimately dehumanizing and alienating them. He also acknowledged some positive aspects of capitalism, both as an improvement on feudalism, but also as a stimulus to improving means of production and economic growth. However, he saw capitalism as just a stage in history— in dialectical terms, as a thesis containing within it an opposing antithesis that would bring about change.

Socialism and communism

Combining his economic analysis of the prevailing capitalist system with a dialectical view of history, Marx developed a basis for his revolutionary political philosophy. The antagonism between capitalists and the proletariat would eventually produce a synthesis, which he believed would culminate in a classless society under communism. This change would be a result of the continued alienation of the workers, but would be precipitated by what he saw as the inherent instability of the capitalist system. While recognizing capitalism's potential for economic growth, Marx pointed out that it was characterized by periodic crises and depressions that cause mass unemployment. These would eventually lead to its collapse, he said, in a revolution transferring power from a "dictatorship of the bourgeoisie" to a "dictatorship of the proletariat" in which means of production would be controlled by the workers. For Marx, this socialist "workers' democracy" was likewise a stage in the progression toward communism, a classless, stateless society with no private property.

The opium of the people

When Kant proposed that the noumenal world is beyond our apprehension (see page 262), he showed that there could be no proof either way for the existence or nonexistence of God. Hegel pointed out our alienation from God, and Feuerbach argued that God was a human creation: the separation of religion from philosophy was almost complete. Marx, who as both a materialist and an atheist argued that theology should be replaced with reason, saw religion as an example of how a class can be made to hold beliefs contrary to their own interests. His famous definition of religion as the "opium of the people" interpreted it as an attempt to find an illusory happiness in the face of oppression and alienation, and called for its abolition, by removing conditions that require illusions and replacing them with those that bring true happiness. This was in line both with Marx's rationalist approach to philosophy and history, and also with the emergence of new disciplines, such as economics, sociology, and psychology, from their philosophical roots using scientific methodology.

Nietzsche: God is dead

Friedrich Nietzsche's philosophy was largely inspired by Schopenhauer, and he agreed with him that the world is driven by an impersonal, aimless Will rather than a supreme being. However, Nietzsche believed there was no more to reality than the world we live in, and that our lives are the only ones we have. Since Plato, many philosophies had included the notion of another world, in some sense superior to the physical one, and most religions held that our lives were precursors to some form of life after death in another "real" world. More than this, our existing morals and values have been shaped by religions, especially the Abrahamic ones of Judaism, Christianity, and Islam, which inherited ideas from ancient Greek philosophy. These, Nietzsche argued, were fine for the societies they originated in, but were no longer relevant to a modern world in which many people no longer subscribed to those old beliefs. Given the claims of materialism, science, and reason, we must accept that this world is all there is, and the old religions are irrelevant; in the modern world, effectively, God is dead.

Man and Superman

Nietzsche proposed that the world we live in is the only reality, and is both godless and aimless. But instead of being horrified and rejecting the world, he believed we should reject the old philosophies and religions and their value systems in order to live our lives to the full. The virtues praised by classical Greek philosophers, and later especially by Christianity, he argued, hold us back from achieving our true potential. We are free to choose the values that are best for us, and should be extolling virtues such as strength and ability rather than humility, which keep us as slaves to a religious value system. By "daring to become what you are," Nietzsche suggested we can free ourselves from this slave morality to go beyond good and evil, and judge the morality of our actions by whether they are life-asserting or not. This "will to power" also allows the emergence of the gifted individual and potential leader, who Nietzsche describes as an *Übermensch*, or "Superman." As the eponymous hero of his *Thus Spoke Zarathustra* says: "Man is something to be surpassed."

Heidegger:
Being and Time

Martin Heidegger was drawn to philosophy by reading the work of Husserl, adopting the methods of phenomenology in his own examination of the nature of existence. Like Husserl, he cut out any discussion of the noumenal world in order to focus on the objects of human experience. Heidegger took this further, however, by pointing out in his book *Being and Time* (1927) that we are aware of our own existence, so it can be examined as part of the phenomenal world. Because it is an object of our experience, our being has to happen somewhere in space. It also exists in time and is inseparable from it—he concluded from our experience of existence having a past, present, and future, that being *is* time. Our lives are framed by time, from birth to death; we come to exist, become aware of our existence, but also become aware that it has an end. Our lives could simply be meaningless, as there are no objective certainties, so our task is to find significance in them. Awareness of death, which Heidegger says is the "furthest horizon of our being," helps us understand our existence and live "authentically."

Existentialism

In the 19th century, some philosophers rejected the objective stance of most philosophy to focus instead on subjective human experience. Søren Kierkegaard was probably the first to identify the feeling of confusion and anxiety when faced with the freedom to make decisions in an apparently meaningless world, and he and later Nietzsche examined the way our choices define the nature of our existence. Although neither called themselves existentialists, their ideas formed the basis for the philosophical approach later known as existentialism. Edmund Husserl's phenomenology, which proposed that we put aside all unanswerable questions and base our philosophy on the world we know was highly influential, particularly on Martin Heidegger, who explained more rigorously the feelings of disorientation first described by Kierkegaard. Phenomenology was further developed by Maurice Merleau-Ponty, and after the Second World War, this subjective philosophical approach was popularized as existentialism in the literary philosophy of Jean-Paul Sartre and Albert Camus.

Existential angst

Arguably the first "existentialist" philosopher (although the term was not adopted until the 20th century), Søren Kierkegaard reacted against Hegel's idea of man as simply a part of a historical process. Instead, he felt that we are free to make the ethical choices that shape our lives, rather than accept the value system passed down to us by society or religion. In his more subjective approach to philosophy, Kierkegaard examined what it is like to be human, and in particular the effect our freedom to make decisions has on our lives. It is the responsibility of each individual, he believed, to give life meaning, and live it to the full. But the realization that we have absolute freedom in our choices is a daunting experience—it creates a feeling of anxiety, what we would now call "existential angst." Kierkegaard describes this "dizziness of freedom" as similar to the vertiginous feelings we have when standing on the edge of a cliff; we fear falling, but also that we may be overcome by a sudden impulse to throw ourselves off, since nothing prevents us from making that choice.

Husserl's phenomenology

Kierkegaard and Nietzsche in their different ways each explored subjective experience in terms of the freedom to make moral decisions to give meaning to life. Edmund Husserl took a more systematic approach, taking the ideas of Kant as a starting point. Kant had shown that we can have no apprehension of things-in-themselves (see page 262), but Husserl felt philosophy had become distracted by unanswerable questions about that noumenal world. He suggested we should put these to one side to concentrate on the "phenomenal" world that we experience. This approach, known as phenomenology, "puts in brackets" the problem of the independent existence of our objects of awareness and examines instead the only things we can be sure of knowing. Husserl called this the *Lebenswelt* ("life's world"). By treating all the objects of our experience as phenomena, and ignoring whether they actually exist or not, we can focus our attention on the first-person experience itself, what it means to be having that experience and the nature of our consciousness.

{Noumena}
(That which we
cannot experience and
cannot apprehend)

Lebenswelt—
the world we
live in

Phenomena
(That which we
experience)

Heidegger: *Being and Time*

Martin Heidegger was drawn to philosophy by reading the work of Husserl, adopting the methods of phenomenology in his own examination of the nature of existence. Like Husserl, he cut out any discussion of the noumenal world in order to focus on the objects of human experience. Heidegger took this further, however, by pointing out in his book *Being and Time* (1927) that we are aware of our own existence, so it can be examined as part of the phenomenal world. Because it is an object of our experience, our being has to happen somewhere in space. It also exists in time and is inseparable from it—he concluded from our experience of existence having a past, present, and future, that being *is* time. Our lives are framed by time, from birth to death; we come to exist, become aware of our existence, but also become aware that it has an end. Our lives could simply be meaningless, as there are no objective certainties, so our task is to find significance in them. Awareness of death, which Heidegger says is the "furthest horizon of our being," helps us understand our existence and live "authentically."

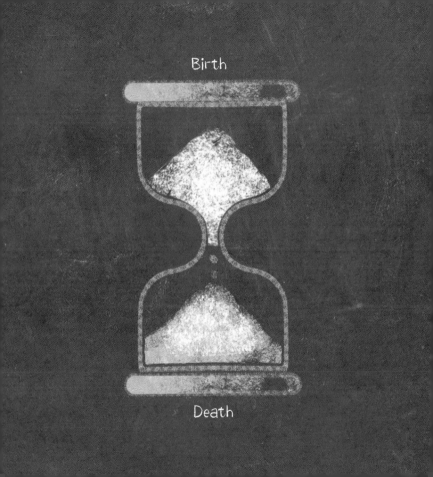

Self-awareness

Heidegger remained a very influential lecturer until he was discredited by his involvement with the Nazi party in the 1930s. Nevertheless, his interpretation of phenomenology in *Being and Time* inspired a generation of philosophers, many of them French, who adopted the term "existentialism." The best known were Sartre and Camus (see pages 308 and 310) —less well known was Maurice Merleau-Ponty, who continued to apply the systematic methods of Husserl and Heidegger's phenomenology to examine subjective human experience. Even more than them, Merleau-Ponty focused on the experience of the individual, each person having his or her own place in space and time. Because we each have a unique existence, reality can only be apprehended from this unique individual perspective. More than that, he argued, we experience not only objects in the world we live in, but also our own existence—we are self-aware. This is what distinguishes the human experience: unlike other material things, we are both subject and object of our awareness.

Self-awareness grants us a unique perspective on reality, but
we must recognize that it is entirely personal and subjective.

Philosophy and literature

A distinctively French approach to philosophy developed in the late 19th century from France's rich literary culture. It was partly influenced by the literary style of philosophers such as Schopenhauer and Nietzsche, and also by the subjective stance of emergent existentialism. In the work of Henri Bergson, the boundary between philosophy and literature was not always clear—indeed, he won the 1927 Nobel Prize in Literature for his philosophical writing. Others, such as Jean-Paul Sartre and Albert Camus, expressed their philosophical ideas in works of literature, popularizing existentialism after the Second World War. Literary criticism also played a part in shaping 20th-century French philosophy, as did the growing fields of linguistics and semiotics (see pages 314 and 316). Structuralists such as Louis Althusser, Jacques Lacan, Michel Foucault, and Jacques Derrida saw philosophical discourse as nothing more than a structure in language. Both existentialism and structuralism became hugely popular worldwide, but were in distinct contrast to mainstream philosophy elsewhere.

Reality as a
perpetual flow

Henri Bergson was deeply influenced by Darwin's theory of evolution, and believed that humans and the world they live in can be understood as part of the evolutionary process. Like Heraclitus (see page 38), he saw reality as a continuous flow: everything is constantly changing and evolving, and the flow of time is fundamental to all reality. As a part of this continuum, we experience it directly, not through our senses or ideas, and the flow of time and our inner experience of it are the same thing. Bergson identified this with the *élan vital* (life force) that he believed drove the process of evolution. In contrast, our perceptions *are* determined by evolution, and our senses are not there to provide us with ideas about the world, but to aid us in our survival. As such, they only tell us what we need to know for survival and do not give an objective picture of the world. We therefore have an incomplete knowledge of the world around us, a relative knowledge from our unique perspective, as compared with the absolute knowledge through direct intuition of the continuum of reality.

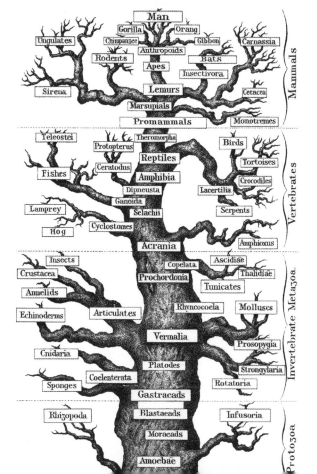

Being and Nothingness

Although he started his career as teacher of philosophy, Jean-Paul Sartre soon became better known as a novelist and playwright. In both literary and philosophical work, however, he explored the ideas of Kierkegaard and Nietzsche concerning freedom to choose value systems and finding meaning in life. His most important philosophical book, *Being and Nothingness* (1943), was also influenced by the phenomenology of Husserl and Heidegger. In it, he explains that we have not been created by a god for a purpose, so we have to create our own purpose in life. By making our own rules and value system, we can determine for ourselves what sort of life we will lead and effectively create ourselves. Existence, he says, precedes essence; first we exist, next we encounter ourselves, and experience "existential angst," then we can create our own essence. It is our choice to do this, and live to the full, or simply accept existing values. Sartre later became involved in communist politics and modified his existentialist views to say that we can never completely free ourselves from the values of society.

"An absurd demand for significance"

Through Sartre's novels and plays, existentialism became popular among the young intellectuals of the 1950s "Beat Generation." Almost as influential were the novels of Sartre's friend Albert Camus, who focused not so much on the freedom to choose implicit in existentialism, but on the meaninglessness of existence. The universe is godless and meaningless, but more than that, it is indifferent to the existence of individual human beings. We feel that our lives should have significance, and search for meaning in our existence, but it is a fruitless search. For Camus, the demand for meaning is absurd. We must learn to accept that there is no meaning to life, but this raises the question whether life is worth living at all—which he saw as the fundamental question of philosophy. Suicide, however, was no answer, merely a surrender. Better, he believed, to embrace the absurdity of existence and rebel against its injustice. Camus's ideas influenced dramatists of the "theater of the absurd" in the later 20th century, including Samuel Beckett (opposite), Eugène Ionesco, Edward Albee, and Tom Stoppard.

The Second Sex

Until the late 20th century, philosophy was almost exclusively a male preserve. The few female philosophers had been overshadowed by their male counterparts, and those who were noticed tended to be political activists more than mainstream philosophers. Simone de Beauvoir, however, took existentialism as a framework for her politics. In *The Second Sex*, she showed that male-dominated society defined what it is to be a woman: man is defined as a human being, but woman as a female. She believed there is a difference between being physically female and the social construct of femininity—"one is not born but becomes a woman." As an existentialist, like her lover Sartre, she believed we are free to choose the values that define us and to create ourselves rather than accept existing norms. Women, therefore, should break free from conventional passive femininity, and also from ideas that they should emulate men, and choose for themselves an authentic existence as women. Written in 1949, *The Second Sex* inspired both the Women's Liberation movement of the 1960s, and "second wave" feminism.

Women's liberation protesters take to the the streets of Washington DC, 1970.

Linguistics and semiotics

Several subjects previously thought of as branches of philosophy emerged as scientific disciplines in the 19th century. As well as psychology, economics, and sociology, thinkers began to apply scientific methods to the study of language. One of the pioneers in this field of "linguistics" was Ferdinand de Saussure, who examined the structure of language and developed a theory that it is made up of "linguistic signs" signifying concepts. This idea became the basis of semiotics, the study of signs and the relationships between the signifier—the sign itself—and the signified—the concept. Analysis of the use of language and signs was given a political dimension by Roland Barthes, who applied semiotic theories to literary criticism and culture in general. As a Marxist, he explained how signs could be used to impose bourgeois cultural values. His scientific approach to the analysis of literature and language, especially with its left-wing tendency, was highly influential on the generation of French philosophers that followed Sartre and Camus, the structuralists.

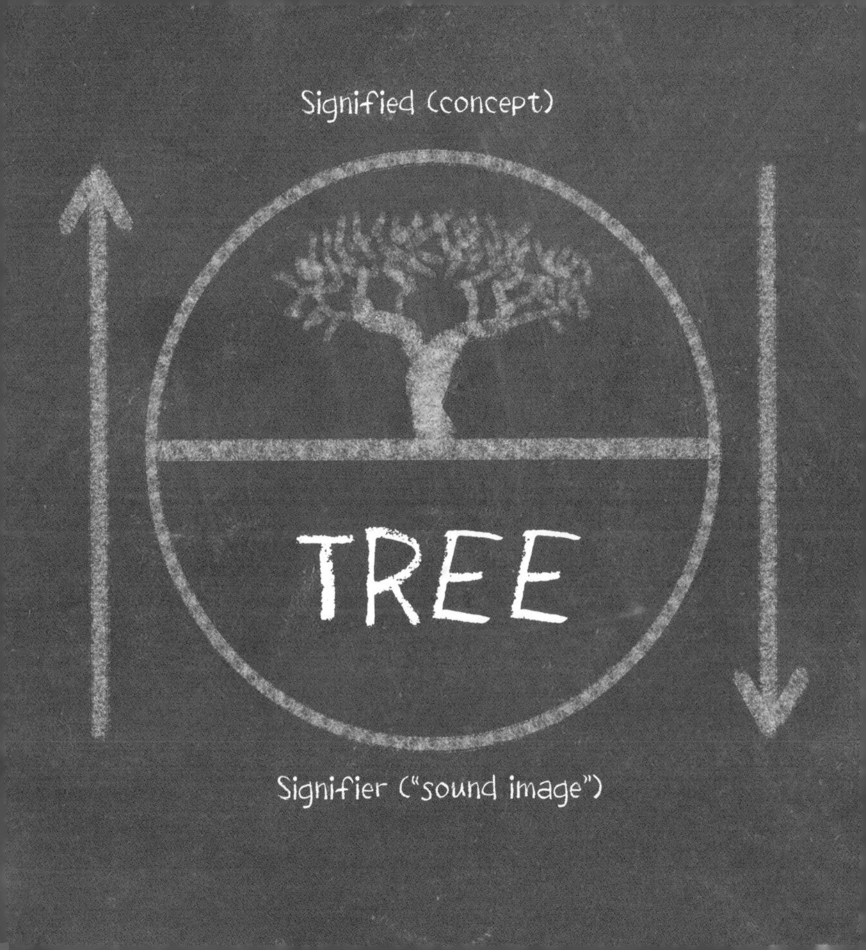
Signified (concept)
TREE
Signifier ("sound image")

Structuralism

Existentialism became the predominant philosophy in France and much of Europe after the Second World War. By the 1960s, however, a rival movement began among French intellectuals. Sartre's Marxism had caused him to modify his ideas of human freedom and choice, and the next generation rejected phenomenology and existentialism completely. Instead, Marxist philosophers such as Louis Althusser saw human behavior as determined by structures, and philosophy as a discourse governed by linguistic structure. Structuralism, as this approach was called, was influenced by the semiotic theories of Barthes, and closely connected to the French tradition of literary criticism. It also informed the psychoanalytic theories of Jacques Lacan and the anthropology of Claude Lévi-Strauss. As it developed in the work of Althusser and Barthes, it was adopted by younger left-wing philosophers such as Michel Foucault and Jacques Derrida. They argued that, since discourse and human behavior are determined by linguistic structures, they, too, can be explained by linguistic analysis.

The structuralist idea that elements of culture must be understood in terms of their relationship to a larger, overarching system or structure influenced many art forms, including architecture.

Deconstruction

Structuralism offered an alternative to existentialism's idea of freedom to choose how we live our lives. However, the notion of structures, especially those modeled on linguistics, shaping our lives was seen as overly deterministic by some. Both Barthes and Foucault had shown how language could be used to impose ideas and exercise power, and rather than having a clear-cut structure and scientific "laws," was open to interpretation. A poststructuralist movement evolved, using a method of analysing language, communication, and discourse known as deconstruction. This was formalized by Derrida in *Of Grammatology* (1967), which included his famous declaration that "there is nothing outside the text," implying that there is no experience of reality, no philosophy, without language. This critical examination of language uncovers not only its deeper meaning, but also its ambiguities. Through deconstruction, poststructuralism uncovered the paradoxical nature of all apparently valid statements about reality or truth, showing them to be based on self-reference and circular reasoning.

Philosophy in the United States

Despite gaining its independence at the end of the 18th century, America retained an essentially European culture. But in the 19th century, an American intellectual tradition emerged, especially in the literary circles of New England. The nonconformist ideas of Ralph Waldo Emerson formed the basis for an idealist philosophy he called transcendentalism —a recognizably American version of Romanticism taken up by authors and poets including Henry Thoreau.

Toward the end of the century, US philosophy became more influenced by scientific thinking. Mathematician Charles Sanders Peirce and psychologist William James were at the forefront of the movement known as pragmatism, which took a practical approach to ideas of knowledge and truth, dismissing philosophizing that has no appreciable effect on our lives. This became the predominant "homegrown" American philosophy of the 20th century, with applications in politics and education explored by figures such as John Dewey and Richard Rorty.

A group of Boston intellectuals including (seated at front) Ralph Waldo Emerson, photographed in 1875.

Transcendentalism

In his 1836 essay *Nature*, Ralph Waldo Emerson set out a philosophy based on the fundamental goodness of both man and nature, similar in some respects to European Romanticism. At its heart was the idea of independence from the prevailing political, social, and religious institutions, replaced with a simple, life of rugged self-reliance in harmony with nature. In that way, individuals could achieve their full potential, and enrich their consciousness. Emerson placed great emphasis on individualism and the possibility that we can each build our own world, discovering for ourselves the meaning of values such as truth and goodness, but he also advocated simple religious faith as practiced by the nonconformist Christians of the time. Among his followers was Henry David Thoreau, who developed the ideas of individualism and nonconformism into an antiestablishment philosophy that verged on anarchism (see page 392). Thoreau also took the simple life to heart, presenting in his book *Walden* (1854) a vision of a community in harmony with nature that anticipates later environmentalism.

WALDEN;

OR,

LIFE IN THE WOODS.

BY HENRY D. THOREAU,

AUTHOR OF "A WEEK ON THE CONCORD AND MERRIMACK RIVERS."

I do not propose to write an ode to dejection, but to brag as lustily as chanticleer in the morning, standing on his roost, if only to wake my neighbors up. — Page 92.

BOSTON:

TICKNOR AND FIELDS.

M DCCC LIV.

Pragmatism

From the scientist's standpoint, philosophical discussion of knowledge, reality, and truth can appear to be merely debate about words, rather than the world we live in. As a mathematician and logician, C.S. Peirce felt that philosophical inquiry often fell into this trap, resulting in conceptions that were not practically useful. He proposed a different approach, using what he later called the pragmatic maxim: "Consider the practical effects of the objects of your conception. Then, your conception of those effects is the whole of your conception of the object." To understand the meaning of something, we should examine whether it makes any difference to a situation or problem—something that has no effect that we can discern with our senses effectively has no meaning for the pragmatist. Pragmatism is concerned not so much with the truth of a statement, as the practical applications of accepting it to be true. Knowledge is not then made up of truths and certainties, but of valid explanations, which can be replaced or improved upon when they are no longer valid or useful.

Consider the practical effects of the objects of your conception. Then, your conception of those effects is the whole of your conception of the object.

(Peirce)

Truth and usefulness

Peirce's pragmatism was enthusiastically taken up by his friend and Harvard University colleague William James. James had a very readable literary style (his brother was the novelist Henry James) and helped to popularize Peirce's ideas, as well as elaborating on them. While Peirce had concerned himself primarily with the meaning of a statement or term, James examined the idea of truth. For him, a statement can be considered true if it provides a valid explanation, allows predictions or gives an insight: if it is useful and does what we require it to do. He gives the example of a man lost in a forest who finds a path: he can choose to believe that it will lead him to safety and follow it out of the forest, or decide that it won't and simply stay where he is and starve. Either way, his action makes his belief true. James makes a distinction between true beliefs, those that are useful to the believer, and facts: "Truths emerge from facts … facts themselves are not true. They simply are. Truth is the function of the beliefs that start and terminate among them."

Philosophy vs. psychology

William James studied medicine before he became a philosopher—a combination of subjects that led to him become a leading figure in the new science of psychology. Pragmatism, with its emphasis on things that make a difference rather than the abstract and speculative, proved complementary to the objective study of human behavior and mental processes. James was among the first true psychologists, helping to mark the field as a scientific discipline through observation, experiments, and analysis of data distinct from the pure reasoning and theorizing of philosophy. He also established the first courses in experimental psychology in the USA. In particular, he worked on a psychological explanation of consciousness, a subject that had long occupied philosophers, but without subjecting it to rigorous scientific scrutiny. Instead, he showed that consciousness is a mental process, a way that we connect and organize our various thoughts. In describing consciousness as a continuous process, James introduced the influential notion of a "stream of consciousness."

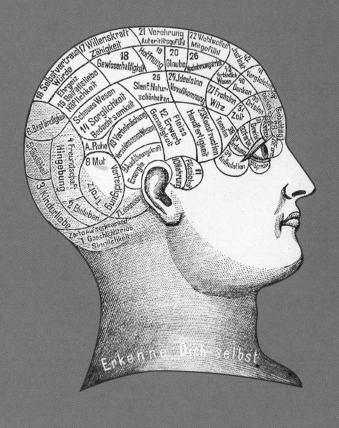

The science of the mind

Psychology evolved from philosophical roots, but set out
to provide a scientific basis for our understanding of the
human mind and behavior. Just as the physical sciences were
beginning to answer questions that had previously been in
the realm of metaphysics, so experimental psychology began
to offer scientific explanations for problems of epistemology
and consciousness. Where philosophers had speculated from
a subjective and often introspective standpoint, psychology
based its explanations on the evidence of not only observation,
but experiment. Behavioral psychologists devised tests to
explore how we acquire knowledge and learn, observing not
only humans but also other animals. Later, cognitive psychology
examined the way our brains process information, and as the
emphasis shifted from "mind" to "brain," psychology moved even
further from philosophical speculation and became more closely
associated with neuroscience. With the advent of computer
technology, the analogy of electronic data processing also
influenced psychological interpretations of the human brain.

Studies of animal behavior offered early clues to the way in which our brains solve problems such as mazes.

Learning by doing

One of the central notions of pragmatism as proposed by Peirce is that knowledge is not about facts, but valid explanations. In the same way as science provides adequate explanations that can be replaced with new or better ones, we acquire knowledge that gives us the information we need for action. The purpose of thinking and learning is to help us do things, and especially to survive in the world, not necessarily to give us an accurate picture of it. John Dewey, one of the next generation of American pragmatists, agreed with Peirce that we learn in order to survive, and that our knowledge comes from participating in, rather than observing, the world we are trying to understand. This process is like a scientific method: we encounter a problem, analyze it, and think of a possible solution, then test it through experiment. Either it works, and the problem is solved, or we have to think of another solution. In fact, we only think when we are confronted with problems, so the best way of acquiring knowledge is through being actively involved in tasks, and not by theorizing or rote learning.

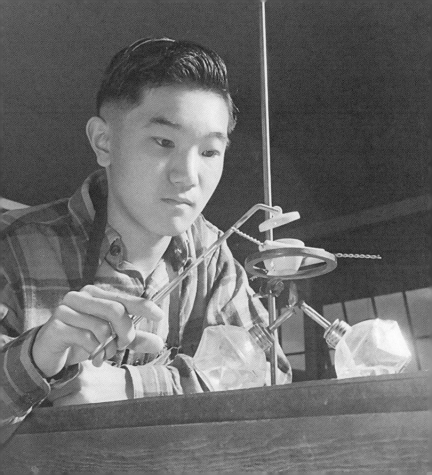

Neopragmatism

For pragmatists, knowledge is concerned not with accurate representation of the world, but with providing adequate explanations. From the late 1960s, working within traditions of pragmatism, but also influenced by European structuralism and poststructuralism, Richard Rorty developed a notion of "neopragmatism" that showed how this is also affected by social and historical context, and closely connected with language. His pragmatic starting point was to reject the idea that knowledge is a "mirror of nature"—that our experience, mediated through reason, delivers a true reflection of the world. He argued that we only become aware of things by *conceptualizing* information from our senses, giving rise to concepts framed in the form of language. We learn, then, through language, and what we consider to be knowledge depends not on how much a statement accurately reflects reality, but on what the society we live in leads us to say. The meaning of a statement or term is not a representation of something in the world, but a product of familiarity and usage.

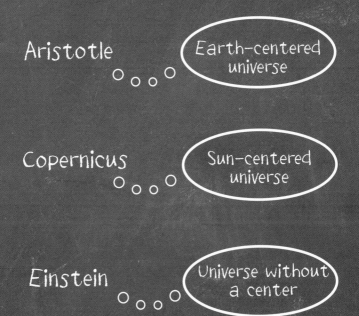

Aristotle, Copernicus, and Einstein offered different conceptions of the universe, but each was an adequate representation for its time.

Modern logic

Logic was established as a branch of philosophy by Greek philosophers and systematically described by Aristotle (see page 84). In the form of the syllogism, it survived virtually unaltered until the late 19th century. Change finally came when mathematicians, notably Gottlob Frege, recognized that logic and mathematics are inseparable, and that mathematics consists of arguments and demonstrations based on logic. This inspired a very British school of thought, analytic philosophy, based on the idea that philosophy, too, is derived from logic. Its leading figure, Bertrand Russell, was the first to analyse the language of philosophical statements as logical propositions. The analytical approach influenced philosophers in the German-speaking world, where it evolved into logical positivism (see page 350), but Russell's influence was seen most importantly in the linguistic philosophy of Ludwig Wittgenstein. Alongside the philosophical analysis of language, however, there was a growing interest in linguistics as a science, which had its own philosophical implications in turn.

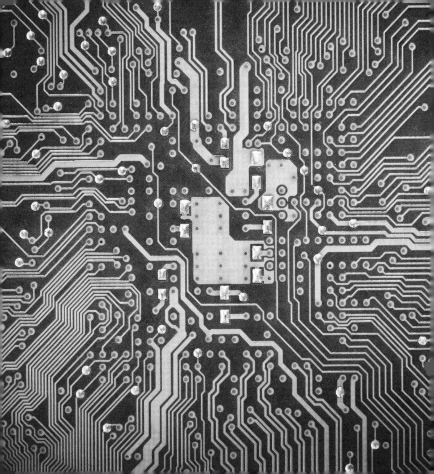

Mathematics and logic

In his book *Begriffsschrift* (1879), German mathematician Gottlob Frege overturned views of logic that had held firm for more than 2,000 years. At the time, it was regarded as a set of "rules" derived from the way that we think. But Frege proposed, for the first time, that logic is objective and has nothing to do with the way we use it. Logical propositions are objective truths, and either follow one from another, or do not, irrespective of human psychology. Frege also pointed out that mathematics consists of a series of arguments and demonstrations to show how one thing follows from another, and therefore has the same principles as logic. Until this point, the prevailing view had been that mathematics, too, was a human creation, like language, but Frege's arguments showed that mathematics was objective and universal. We do not create it, but discover it in the same way that we discover physical laws. Frege's linking of mathematics and logic also showed that there was far more to logic than the syllogism, making it a more powerful tool for philosophy.

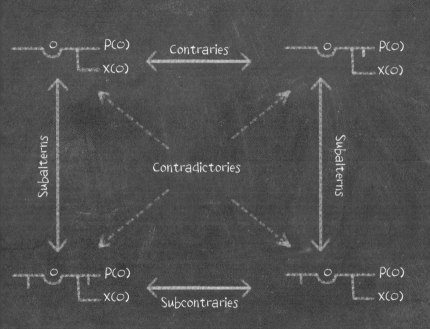

In his *Begriffsschrift*, Frege developed a complex system of conceptual notation for analysing philosophical problems. Here, his notations applied to the standard arguments of the syllogism (see page 84).

Logic vs. epistemology

Frege's insight that logic is not a creation of the human mind, but consists of universal objective truths, had profound implications for philosophy. Mathematics, he said, followed the same principles as logic, and so was equally objective. But the process of reasoning that underlies philosophy is also a series of arguments and demonstrations, governed by logical principles and is similarly not a human creation. Philosophical truths should therefore be objective, and discoverable in the same way that we can discover the truths of mathematics, independent of the way our minds work.

Much of modern philosophy, however, has been based on epistemology, the study of how we know, what we know, and what we *can* know, all of which concerns what is going on in our minds and is effectively irrelevant to philosophical truth. For philosophy to discover objective truths about our knowledge, it now became clear, it must have its foundations in logic, not epistemology.

Principia Mathematica

Frege's work went virtually unnoticed outside a small circle of mathematicians, and was ignored by philosophers until it was discovered by Bertrand Russell. Russell had studied both philosophy and mathematics at Cambridge University and had independently concluded that arithmetic, and possibly all of mathematics, could be derived from logic, stating the case in *Principles of Mathematics* (1903). He and his colleague Alfred North Whitehead then attempted to prove this in the massive three-volume *Principia Mathematica*, completed ten years later. Following this, he turned his attention fully to philosophy, unsurprisingly concentrating on logic (and probably influenced in this choice by his godfather, John Stuart Mill, who had written the definitive 19th-century book on the subject). Like Frege, Russell recognized the implications of breakthroughs in logic and mathematics for philosophy. They had shown that logic is an objective set of universal truths, and Russell believed that with science and philosophy both based on logic, we should be able to discover an objective knowledge of the world.

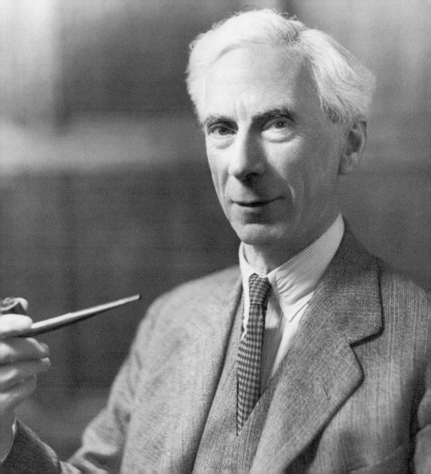

Analytic philosophy

Russell came from the tradition of empiricism and, along with his colleague G.E. Moore, led the British movement in philosophy away from the idealism that had dominated the 19th century. Having demonstrated that mathematics and logic were inseparably connected in the *Principia* (see page 342), Russell set out to show that logic should be the basis for philosophical inquiry: because it consists of objective, universal truths, logic is a firmer foundation for our knowledge of the world than the speculation offered by epistemology. Applying techniques of logical analysis to statements about our knowledge enables an objective evaluation of them, an approach to philosophical inquiry that became known as analytic philosophy. In order to analyse philosophical statements logically, they first have to be presented in a logical form, similar to the propositions of mathematics, using the formal grammar and signs and symbols of logic. A philosophical argument can then be shown as valid or invalid using the rules of logic, in much the same way as a mathematical proof.

$$\exists x \forall y (\phi(y) \iff y = x \land \psi(y))$$

Truth and logic

Analytic philosophy offered the prospect of a more scientific method of examining philosophical arguments. Translating them into a series of logical propositions, however, can be problematic. Before their validity can be tested, the sometimes flowery and convoluted language of philosophers must be presented as simply as possible, but the concepts of philosophy are frequently not as clear-cut as those in a mathematical or logical proposition and, unlike numbers and symbols, words and phrases present problems of meaning, so it is sometimes impossible to establish the truth of a statement. Seemingly similar statements in the same logical form, may have very different logical implications. For example, if we say, "The King of Spain is bald," the meaning is clear and we can check the facts to establish empirically if it is true or false. However, the statement "The King of France is bald" has exactly the same logical form, and an obvious meaning, but is it true or false? There *is* no King of France, so how can we check? Despite its valid logical form, such a statement may have no meaning at all.

Most unicorns are white.

Tractatus Logico-Philosophicus

As a student of Russell, Ludwig Wittgenstein adopted the principles of analytic philosophy, then set out to establish the limits of our knowledge using logic in the same way that Kant and Schopenhauer had previously used epistemology. In *Tractatus Logico-Philosophicus* (1921), he showed that in trying to understand the world, we describe it using language that consists of propositions with logical structures: "The totality of propositions is language." The world, "the totality of facts, not things," is also structured, and language pictures the world by making a representation, or "map," in the same logical form as the world it describes. All that can be meaningfully said is "the totality of true propositions," statements that can be empirically verified about the phenomenal world of experience. Philosophy should confine itself to this world, since language limits the things it can meaningfully discuss, in effect, to statements about natural science. Subjects such as ethics and religion are still important, Wittgenstein said, but are "mystical"—we can make no meaningful propositions about them.

Logical positivism

Thanks to Russell, Frege's work on logic reached a wider readership. By the 1920s, it was not only British thinkers who incorporated the new logic into their philosophy: a group of scientists and mathematicians known as the Vienna Circle formed with the aim of establishing a philosophical basis for science. They believed that it is the job of science, not philosophy, to provide truths about the world, but the job of philosophy is to provide a logical framework in which science can work. The view they developed, logical positivism, applied the techniques of logic to the statements of science in the same way that analytic philosophy approached philosophical statements. To talk clearly and objectively about scientific ideas and theories, we must first analyse the language of scientific statements as logical propositions to ascertain their meaning, ruling out any that are meaningless. For the logical positivist, a statement can be accepted as true only if it meets strict logical criteria and can be empirically verified; anything else cannot be proved and so is effectively meaningless.

Founded by philosopher Moritz Schlick (left) in 1922, the Vienna Circle also included mathematician Hans Hahn and sociologist, economist and philosopher Otto Neurath.

Language as a tool

By the mid-20th century, analytic philosophy had become the predominant philosophy of the English-speaking world. Logical positivism was also influential, as members of the Vienna Circle fled from Nazism to Britain and the United States, and its strict criteria of meaningfulness were applied to all forms of language, not just science. Analytic philosophy had become largely an analysis of language, rather than of philosophical questions. But not all British philosophers accepted this trend, and some, such as G.E. Moore, argued for a "common sense" approach to logical analysis of language. Wittgenstein also returned to the argument, realizing that his *Tractatus* was self-contradictory: it was full of propositions that do not picture the world, and so are meaningless. In its place, he developed an entirely different linguistic philosophy, dropping the metaphor of language "picturing" reality and replacing it with language as a tool. Each word or concept does not mean a specific thing, but derives its meaning from the intention of its user and the context in which it is used.

Linguistics

Both British and continental philosophy became increasingly concerned with language as the 20th century progressed. Analytic philosophy called for the analysis of philosophical statements to render them in a logical form, prompting an interest in the philosophy of language itself, while in France the tradition of literary philosophy spawned structuralism, a philosophy based on linguistic structure. This trend was mirrored in the growth of linguistics itself. The aim of this young science was to study language using scientific methods, but there was also some cross-fertilization with linguistic philosophy. Among other things, linguistics is concerned with the structure of language, in terms of its grammar, semantics, and so on, and this influenced the structuralist movement. It also studies the way that languages have evolved, how they differ from one another, and whether there is an underlying structure common to all languages. This, too, has philosophical implications, in particular in the study of the way that we acquire language and use it to express our ideas.

jezik limbă הפשה język la langue

dil linguagem kieli език اللغة

язык **language** taal

idioma 言語 tungumál γλώσσα

kalba језика språk bahasa

lingua sprache lugha lingwa 언어

Universal grammar

One of the questions that occupied linguistics was whether there is a common grammatical structure to all human languages. There are families of related languages that share similar grammars but the many different families seem to have little or nothing in common. An answer to this problem came from Noam Chomsky, later better known for his critical analysis of political power (see page 384). He noticed that children become proficient in their mother tongue far more quickly than one might expect from the amount of stimulus they are given, and regardless of the particular language a child is learning. Chomsky concluded that we must have some innate knowledge of the structure of language, and that this structure must be common to all languages—a universal or "generative" grammar. The notion of language having a universal formal structure was analogous to the link between logic and mathematics, but the idea of an *a priori* understanding of it harked back to Cartesian rationalism and was difficult to square with linguistics' claim to be a scientific discipline in the empiricist tradition.

Artificial intelligence

Advances in science and technology have produced machines capable of performing tasks that previously could only be done by human thought. Sophisticated computer programing has taken them beyond the realm of simple calculation, and given them "artificial intelligence," including the ability to use language. So machines can mimic human behavior—but can they actually think? Mathematician and computer pioneer Alan Turing proposed a simple test of a machine's ability to show intelligence. A machine and a human are both asked questions in normal human language, to which they give replies in the same language. If an impartial judge cannot tell which answers are which, the machine has passed the test and is considered to be showing intelligence. Modern computers are increasingly able to do this successfully, especially as we program them to process information in the same way as human brains and even introduce such concepts as "fuzzy logic." But can we therefore say that they are capable of "thinking"? Will they ever be capable of what we understand to be consciousness?

Experimental setup for a Turing test

1 Human questioner

2 Terminals to display responses

3 Barrier

4 Human answerer

5 Computer

6 Experiment controller relays either human or computer response

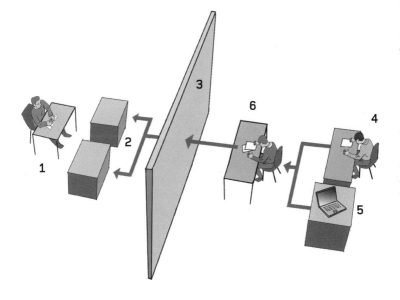

Philosophy and science in the 20th century

Most of the sciences evolved from branches of philosophy, complementing them with scientific theories describing the physical world. But as the pace of progress accelerated with the scientific revolution of the Enlightenment, the natural sciences largely replaced metaphysics, and by the end of the 19th century psychology and neuroscience began to provide a scientific alternative to the philosophy of the mind. In the 20th century, Albert Einstein's theories seemed to provide a comprehensive explanation of the physical universe, but many aspects of the new physics threw up almost as many questions as answers—problems that science alone could not explain. And just as science appeared to be replacing aspects of philosophy, some philosophers turned their attention to science itself. Karl Popper proposed a practical answer to the problem of induction (see page 226), the basis of scientific methods, while Paul Feyerabend questioned the notion of a single reliable scientific method, based on Thomas Kuhn's idea that science makes advances not in a smooth progression, but in a radical jumps.

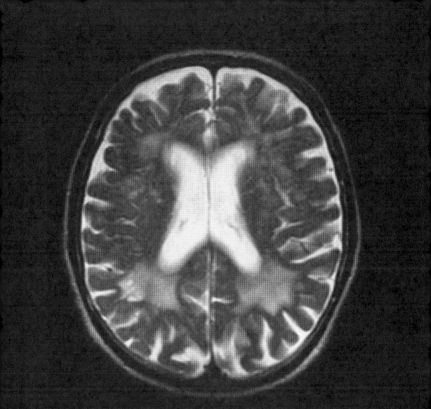

Neuroscience can tell us more about the way our brains
work than introspective philosophy.

Scientific answers to metaphysical questions

When Einstein formulated his theories of relativity at the beginning of the 20th century, he ushered in a completely new way of understanding the universe. This overturned the old Newtonian view, replacing it with a comprehensive description of the physical universe according to a new set of physical laws. For the first time, time and space themselves were explained scientifically, and the substance of the universe was defined in terms of energy. Many of the metaphysical questions that had concerned philosophy from its earliest beginnings seemed finally to be answered. But, as Einstein would have happily admitted, the new physics was not a definitive answer, nor did it negate the importance of Newton's contribution. It was not "right" or "true," but simply a more accurate explanation than Newton's, which was perfectly good for its time—as a pragmatist would say, it was a valid explanation. And just as Newtonian physics marked a stage in the history of science, so too Einstein's theories might one day be replaced with something that fits the facts even better.

Einstein's famous equation shows that energy (E) is equal to the product of mass (m) and the square of the speed of light (c).

New philosophical questions

While Einstein's theories appeared to bring an end to a lot of metaphysical speculation, the physics that he pioneered also posed fresh questions. And rather than disproving old philosophical theories, it appeared to confirm or at least complement many. The definition of matter as energy, for example, has more than a superficial resemblance to the idealism of Schopenhauer or even Hindu and Buddhist philosophy. Many of the concepts of quantum mechanics, meanwhile, are hard for even physicists to understand, and seem almost mystical—such as Heisenberg's uncertainty principle and the "observer effect" (the necessity of observation in "fixing" the properties of a microscopic quantum system), which seem to defy common sense, but have an uncanny resemblance to Berkeley's philosophy. The Big Bang theory of the origin of the universe, meanwhile, also reopened the philosophical debate about the nature of reality and causality—and the possibility that there is more than one universe presents even more food for philosophical thought.

Quite apart from the scientific import of the famous "Schrödinger's cat" thought experiment, what are the philosophical implications of a cat being simultaneously alive and dead?

Falsifiability

The method science uses to establish theories is based on induction—inferring a general rule from individual instances. Even after Hume pointed that induction cannot logically be used to show anything with certainty (see page 226), scientists continued to use the methods of observation and experiment with remarkable success. But the problem of induction still nagged philosophers until the 1930s, when Karl Popper proposed a different way of viewing scientific methodology. He argued that while vast numbers of positive instances of an event cannot prove a scientific theory conclusively, a single negative instance can decisively show it to be false. As an example, he gave the hypothesis: "All swans are white"; this cannot be proved true by reference to any number of observations of white swans, but can be proved false or "falsified" by the appearance of just one black swan. The true criterion of a scientific theory is not that it is inferred by induction, but that it should be falsifiable, capable of being shown as false by observation or experiment.

Paradigm shifts

The philosophy of science developed in the 20th century as an important branch in its own right, especially after Karl Popper's groundbreaking work. As well as examining the philosophical and logical basis of scientific methodology, philosophers turned their attention to the nature of scientific progress. It had been assumed that advances in science were a process of continuous evolution, until in 1962 Thomas Kuhn introduced the notion of paradigm shifts. In his analysis of the history of science, he suggested that periods of "normal" science are interrupted by periods of "crisis." During the periods of normality, scientists work within an agreed framework, or paradigm, and any anomalies in their work are overlooked or dismissed. If, however, the anomalies become significant, this provokes a crisis, in which they have to be accounted for by new theories and a shift to a new paradigm. Normal science now resumes under the new framework, until the next crisis. Historical examples of such paradigm shifts include the revolutionary theories of Copernicus, Newton, and Einstein.

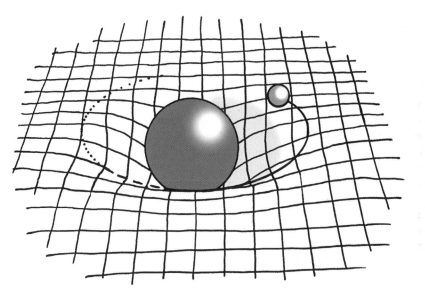

Newton's ideas of gravity served as a framework for more than 200 years, but were overturned by Einstein's general theory of relativity, which is almost universally accepted by modern science.

Against Method

Kuhn's depiction of the history of scientific progress as a series of periodic revolutions was given an anarchistic spin by his friend Paul Feyerabend. When a paradigm shift occurs, all the accepted concepts are affected and so, Feyerabend argued in 1975, there is no single, permanent framework for establishing scientific truth. New approaches and methods are adopted and become the consensus of scientists, but they would not have been considered valid before. Scientific progress, therefore, is not achieved by following strict rules— on the contrary, advances are made when these are broken. Feyerabend rejected attempts to justify the scientific method as Popper had done, proposing that there are no universal methodological rules and attempts to find such rules hinder scientific progress. In particular, he attacked the criterion of consistency with known facts, pointing out that no major theory was consistent with an older one covering the same ground. If science is to continue to advance, he argued, it would do better to ignore any prescriptive theories of methodology.

New Edition

AGAINST METHOD

Paul Feyerabend

Introduced by Ian Hacking

Twentieth-century political philosophy

The 20th century saw unprecedented changes in the world's political makeup. Around a third of the world adopted some form of Marxist-inspired regime, while old European colonial empires shrank. Mid-century, the rise of tyrannical fascism and Nazism sparked the Second World War, followed by the Cold War between Eastern communism and Western capitalism. Political philosophy reacted in various ways to these changes, suggesting new models to replace the failing systems. The harsh reality of communist regimes prompted a reappraisal of Marx's theories in the 1930s, and again after the collapse of the Soviet Union in the 1990s. In the US, philosophers concentrated on notions of democracy, justice, and the role of government, ideas that were also of importance to the many states seeking and gaining independence from colonial rule. In the comparatively peaceful period following 1945, issues of civil rights, including race and gender, and pressing environmental problems also played a significant role in shaping modern political philosophy.

US and Soviet tanks face off against each other in postwar Berlin at the beginning of the Cold War that shaped much of political philosophy in the 20th century.

The Frankfurt School

Almost 70 years after the *Communist Manifesto*, Marx's ideas of a socialist state were made real by the formation of the Soviet Union. Marxist political philosophy was gaining followers worldwide and other countries were soon to follow suit. But some Marxist philosophers, especially in Europe, felt that communism was beginning to lose sight of the core values of Marxism and were as critical of apologists for the Soviet regime under Stalin as they were of capitalism.

A group of thinkers, initially based at the Institute for Social Research at the University of Frankfurt, formed to establish a new form of Marxism bringing in ideas from sociology, psychology, and existentialist philosophy. Leading figures of the so-called Frankfurt School (a term of convenience for a group that were only loosely connected) included philosophers Max Horkheimer, Walter Benjamin, Herbert Marcuse, and Theodor Adorno; among the next generation who further developed these ideas were Jürgen Habermas and György Lukács.

Key members of the Frankfurt School including Horkheimer and Adorno (front left and right).

Critical theory

The neo-Marxist philosophy that emerged from the Frankfurt School may have seemed quite radical for its time, but had its roots in 19th-century German philosophical ideas. At its core was the idea of "critical theory" (not to be confused with the theory of literary criticism that bears the same name), which was ultimately derived from Kant's notion of providing a critique of existing ideas. More importantly, however, critical theory harked back to Hegel's dialectic (see page 276) and Marx's exhortation to philosophers not to describe or explain the world, but to change it. Philosophers of the Frankfurt School sought to challenge ideologies, in particular those that imposed a world view designed to perpetuate the status quo, such as capitalism and the form of communism that had evolved in the 20th century. A rigorous critique of the existing systems, using theories of sociology and psychology as well as philosophy, could be used to analyse political and social structures in order to produce a synthesis that could transform society for the better.

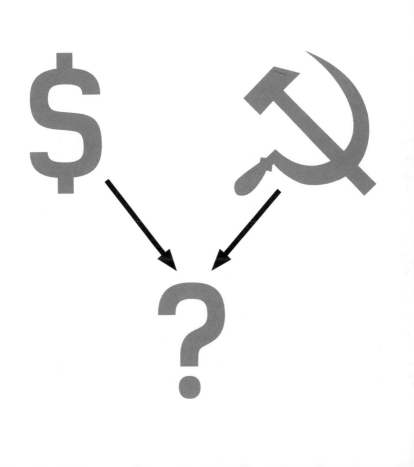

Pragmatism
and democracy

For John Dewey, philosophy and politics were inextricably linked. He saw his own pragmatism (see page 324) as a philosophical basis for democracy. For too long, he believed, thinkers had dealt with "the problems of philosophers," abstract notions of metaphysics, and epistemology, when their attention should be on "the problems of men." So long as political philosophy continued to be divorced from experience, people had no influence on the institutions controlling their lives. Pragmatism not only overcame this with its focus on the usefulness of knowledge, but Dewey's emphasis on active acquisition of knowledge necessitated democracy as the political system. Democratic society, he argued, is not formed by the imposition of a social contract, but is an organic aggregate of individual citizens, and can only grow and evolve if individuals, too, are free to grow and evolve. The aim of democracy is therefore to provide the conditions for this, and the function of his philosophy is to establish a "moral community," largely through education, in which individuals can achieve this self-realization.

Justice as fairness

One of the central concerns of Socrates's discussions in the time of the classical Greek philosophers was the definition of justice, and in the 1970s philosophers revisited this idea in the light of American capitalist democracy. Among them was John Rawls, who put the case for liberalism with his definition of "justice as fairness." In explanation, Rawls described a thought experiment known as the "veil of ignorance," in which participants create an imaginary society from scratch—an "original position"—and choose the distribution of rights, resources, and positions in the society they will then live in. However, the veil of ignorance prevents them from knowing anything about their own abilities, intelligence, social standing, or wealth, so personal considerations of their own place in the new society do not affect their judgment. They are forced to consider the new society from the perspective of benefit to *all* members of the society, regardless of their standing, and justice is achieved by a fair distribution.

Justice as entitlement

In response to Rawls's liberal definition of justice as fairness, Robert Nozick offered an alternative definition that better fitted his libertarian views. Justice, for Nozick, is a matter of entitlement. Influenced by the economic theories of Friedrich Hayek and the political philosophy of Locke, his entitlement theory has three main principles: justice in acquisition (how a person first comes to own property), justice in transfer (how a person can acquire property from another person with their consent, by trade or as a gift), and rectification of injustice (how to deal with property that is acquired or transferred unjustly). Distribution of property is just when everyone is entitled to the property they possess: anyone who acquires property according to the principles of justice in acquisition or justice in transfer is entitled to it, but no one is entitled to property acquired in other ways, and rectification exists to deal with cases such as theft or fraud. State intervention should be limited to protection of entitlement, and redistribution without consent, for example through taxation, is unjust.

Analysis of political power

Although much political philosophy is concerned with theories of the ideal state and arguments about the role of government within such a state, it may also cast a critical eye over existing political systems. Noam Chomsky had been attracted to left-wing and anarchist politics from an early age, and after making his name in linguistics (see page 356) turned his attention to political philosophy. As a moral philosopher, he believed in applying the same standards of morality to ourselves as to other people, and in politics we should do likewise, examining the morality of all states, especially our own. We have a tendency to assume our home state acts more ethically than others, because we examine not the actions, but the rhetoric of our own government, and find it easier to accept it than question whether it is being put into practice. In any state, however, there is a discrepancy between the government's political claims and its actions, and this is no less true for the state we happen to live in, so we must make an objective analysis of the way our government exerts political power.

The failure of the left

A perennial concern for left-wing political philosophers from the Frankfurt School onward has been the continued success of capitalism, despite Marx's prediction of its inevitable collapse. After the failure of Soviet socialism in the Eastern Bloc, few states continued to follow any form of Marxist socialism or communism—even China developed its own version of a mixed economy. Marxist thinkers found themselves in opposition, and powerless. This was seen by Slavoj Žižek as providing something of an easy way out, however, since it allowed them to adopt a stance of resistance, theorizing about an ideal state without the responsibility of putting it into practice, and ignoring Marx's own exhortation for philosophers to stop interpreting the world and start changing it. The real failure of the left, Žižek says, is to have given up on overthrowing capitalism and opted to continue talking about the elusive society it could have created. Instead, there should be a reevaluation of revolutionary socialism in the light of what happened, and exploitation of capitalism's increasing failures.

Environmentalism

Concern for the environment, in the industrialized world at least, had only a small role in philosophy until the 19th century. The Romantic preoccupation with Nature and the American transcendentalist ideal of living in harmony with it, were partly reactions to industrialization, but the idea that humans form only a part of the natural world is also present in the philosophy of Schopenhauer (see page 270). Ideas from the new science of ecology were taken up by philosophers such as Arne Naess, who showed that we have a responsibility for the long-term preservation of a world that does not exist simply for our own benefit. Irresponsible use of resources reduces their future availability and pollutes the environment, endangering all life including our own. Naess urged us to recognize our relationship to the biosphere and "think like a mountain," not only to prevent harm to the natural world, but also to live a more meaningful life. His ideas were influential on the growing political Green movement, which gained momentum as the threat of climate change became increasingly difficult to ignore.

Race and philosophy

Despite American political philosophy's preoccupation with democracy, African-Americans remained second-class citizens even after the Civil War and abolition of slavery. The struggle for civil rights was spearheaded by W.E.B. Du Bois, founder of the National Association for the Advancement of Colored People (NAACP) in 1909, and culminated with Martin Luther King's political campaign in the 1960s, making race and racism important issues for political philosophy. Black American thinkers also helped encourage African nations in their struggle for independence. Martinique-born existentialist Frantz Fanon was among the first postcolonial African philosophers, and emphasized the idea of a nation choosing an identity for itself. Many newly independent nations opted to model themselves on Western democracies, others chose Marxist-inspired socialist republics—but underlying all was a sense of freedom from European rule. Later, a distinctly African philosophical movement evolved, incorporating traditional ideas, but highlighting issues of poverty and deprivation, as well as race and oppression.

Civil disobedience

It almost goes without saying that individuals often disagree with the policies of their governments—especially if that government is tyrannical or an exploitative colonial power. But what if the individual considers the state's actions morally wrong? The transcendentalist Henry Thoreau (see page 322) believed that laws suppress rather than protect the civil liberties of the citizen, and saw it as a citizen's right to resist any laws to which he or she had a conscientious objection. He advocated peaceful resistance through noncooperation—in his own case the nonpayment of taxes that would support the slave trade and the war in Mexico. To passively permit laws and government policies that are against our moral beliefs is to effectively validate them, so it is not only our right but our duty to resist them. Thoreau's idea of the moral rightness of civil disobedience on the grounds of conscience, and especially the use of nonviolent resistance, was adopted successfully by Gandhi in the fight for Indian independence, and by Martin Luther King in the struggle for civil rights in the United States.

Gender and philosophy

The "second-wave" feminism of the 1950s and 60s was inspired by Simone de Beauvoir's assertion that femininity is imposed on women by society (see page 312). As well as the political Women's Liberation movement, there was considerable discussion by feminist philosophers, that continued into a so-called "third wave" from the 1990s onward. In the tradition of continental philosophy, this used poststructuralism and deconstruction to analyse discourse about and by women, in order to ascertain how male-dominated culture, including philosophy, shapes the way women are viewed and the way they view themselves. But there was also some debate as to whether notions of gender are purely social constructs or whether there is in fact an intrinsic difference between the sexes beyond the purely physical. Gender studies emerged as a separate discipline, considering the role of sexuality in determining gender difference. The gradual acceptance of other sexualities at the time complicated the debate, since these did not fit neatly into traditional gender definitions.

Applied philosophy

In the face of ever-more successful and comprehensive scientific explanations of the world, the fields of metaphysics and epistemology have gradually received less attention from philosophers. The emphasis in late 20th-century philosophy shifted to moral philosophy and ethics, and especially political philosophy. Another recent change has been in the role that philosophy plays in society. For much of its history, Western philosophy has been the realm of the intelligentsia, viewed as an "ivory-tower" academic discipline even in the modern era, but today the relevance of moral philosophy in particular has been recognized. Practical applications of philosophical ideas have been found not only in politics and the law, but also in business, economics, science, and medicine, especially in the ethics of decision-making in those areas. Logic, too, has its place in analysing the validity of arguments in many spheres of life. Philosophers today are not only found in university departments, but also employed for their expertise by governments, health authorities, and corporations.

Questions of moral philosophy, and decisions of right and wrong, are a fundamental part of what happens in the courtroom.

Politics, economics, and business ethics

Political philosophy can be seen as the application of moral philosophy to the practical question of the sort of society we want to live in. Economics also emerged from philosophy, before becoming a scientific study of resource management. Both have dealt with issues such as the distribution of wealth, public and private goods, and the laws that protect rights and freedoms, but more recently, philosophy has been called upon to consider the ethics of decisions in the worlds of commerce and finance. What, for example, are a company's responsibilities to its shareholders, customers, and employees? Should institutions like banks be trying to make profits or providing a service to society? Issues of exploitation have also been brought to center stage: cheap labor in the developing world brings down prices for the consumer, but is morally dubious, and could cause unemployment at home; companies supplying products such as tobacco and even junk food could be accused of exploiting their customers; and exploitation of natural resources raises a host of questions of environmental ethics.

Scientific and medical ethics

Advances in science and medicine are usually regarded as mainly beneficial to society, but some have opened up a whole new field of ethical discussion. New discoveries in medicine, for example, have improved both the length and quality of life, which on the face of it is clearly morally good. Nevertheless, we must weigh up their benefits against issues such as animal testing, human embryo research, the morality of commercial drug companies, and so on. Medical procedures such as abortion and the thorny problem of euthanasia also pose ethical dilemmas that are far from clear-cut. Just about every area of scientific research involves decisions that have a moral dimension: genetically modified crops, cloning, energy production, and especially weapons research are all areas that require ethical scrutiny. There is also the question of cost—money spent on projects such as space exploration or particle accelerators is difficult enough to justify in simple economic terms, but can it be morally justified when so much of the world's population is living in extreme poverty?

Philosophy and education

Philosophers throughout history, particularly in the areas of moral and political philosophy, have often recognized the importance of education. Epistemology, the study of knowledge and its acquisition, has also influenced the development of educational techniques, and some of the most influential educational theorists, including Jean Piaget and John Dewey, have approached the subject from a philosophical angle.

The philosophy of education considers not only the methodology of teaching and learning, but also the purpose of education and what is being taught. For philosophers from Plato onward, education was seen as a means of instilling moral values, guiding students in the way they should lead their lives, and the sort of society they should live in. This has been the primary ethos of education until comparatively recently, but in the modern world, is it the place of schools and colleges to provide moral education, or should they solely teach skills for working life, enabling students to become productive members of society?

Science vs. religion

From its ancient Greek beginnings, Western philosophy set out to find rational explanations for things that were previously explained by religion. With the advent of Christianity, however, there was an uneasy relationship between reasoning and matters of faith, as philosophy challenged Church dogma. But it was "natural philosophy"—what we now call science— that posed the greatest threat to the dominance of religion, and from the Renaissance onward there was an increasing reliance on scientific explanations of the universe. By the 20th century, philosophers had generally accepted there can be no proof of the existence of God, and atheism became an acceptable standpoint. Western society has become generally more secular in recent years, Yet despite this, around three-quarters of the world still identify themselves as believers in some religion, and some fundamentalists, such as creationists, even reject scientific evidence in favor of divine revelation. Science may be vitally necessary to the modern world, but it would seem that religion is at least equally important.

The future of philosophy

What is the place of philosophy in a world so dominated by science and technology? Many philosophical explanations of the world have been superseded by scientific theories, and the areas of metaphysics, epistemology, and logic have been explored apparently to their limits. Twenty-first-century philosophers have become more concerned with moral and political questions, and the trend to practical applications seems set to continue. But in philosophy there are, more often than not, no definitive answers. Many problems have still not been satisfactorily tackled, and some of our assumptions may yet be proved entirely wrong. It may be that even science, philosophy's brilliant offspring, could reveal fundamental flaws. Philosophers are still unraveling the implications of their predecessors' ideas and building on their legacy, but the recent revival in philosophy has attracted a new generation of thinkers. If history is any guide, there is no doubt that another Socrates, Descartes, Hume, or Kant will emerge from among them with a revolutionary new idea to change forever the way we think.

Glossary

Aesthetics
The branch of philosophy concerned with the nature of art and beauty, the arts, artistic values, and criticism.

Analytic philosophy
An approach to philosophy based on logical analysis of statements and arguments to clarify their meaning and establish whether they provide objective knowledge of the world.

Analytic statement
A statement that can be shown to be true or false by analyzing it without reference to other facts. It is the opposite of a synthetic statement, whose truth can only be determined by checking the facts it refers to.

A priori and *a posteriori*
A proposition is *a priori* if it is known to be true without evidence from experience. Propositions that can only be known to be true by experience are *a posteriori*.

Contingent
A contingent truth is one that happens to be true, but in other circumstances might not have been. A necessary truth, on the other hand, is one that is true in any circumstances, and could not be otherwise.

Cosmos
(*see* World)

Deduction
A process of inference drawing a particular conclusion from a general premise. For example, "All men are mortal. Socrates is a man. Therefore Socrates is mortal." In contrast, induction infers from the particular to the general. For example, "Socrates, Plato, and Aristotle were

philosophers. They were all Greek. Therefore all philosophers are Greek." If the premises of a deductive argument are true, the conclusion is also true, but in an inductive argument the conclusion may or may not be true.

Determinism
The view that every event is determined by and the necessary outcome of a prior cause, and that nothing can happen other than what happens.

Dialectic
In the philosophy of Hegel and Marx, the idea that any statement, action, or state contains within it a contradiction that provokes

opposition, and results in a synthesis that reconciles the two.

Dualism
The view that things are made up of two different elements. In the philosophy of mind, dualism refers to the view that mind and body are distinct.

Empiricism
The view that all knowledge is acquired through experience, and there is no such thing as *a priori* knowledge.

Epistemology
The branch of philosophy concerned with knowledge— what, if anything, we can know, how we acquire knowledge, and what knowledge is.

Ethics
The branch of philosophy concerned with how we should live our lives and morality, including questions of right and wrong, good and bad, and duty.

Existentialism
An approach to philosophy based on the subjective human experience of existence, and in particular the search for meaning in life.

Fallacy
An error of reasoning or false conclusion.

Falsifiability
In the philosophy of Popper, the concept that a theory is capable of being proved false by empirical evidence.

Humanism

The approach that considers humankind as more important than any supernatural world as a basis for philosophical inquiry.

Idealism

The view that reality is ultimately immaterial, and consists of minds, ideas, or spirits. The opposite of materialism.

Induction

(*see* Deduction)

Inference

A process of reasoning in which a conclusion follows from premises, such as deduction and induction.

Logic

The branch of philosophy concerned with the methods, rules, and validity of rational argument.

Materialism

The view that reality is ultimately material or physical, and consists of matter. Materialism is therefore the opposite of idealism.

Metaphysics

The branch of philosophy concerned with the nature of reality, of what exists, including concepts of being and substance.

Monism

The view that things are made up of a single element.

Moral philosophy

(*see* Ethics)

Necessary

(*see* Contingent)

Noumenon

The reality, also known as the "thing-in-itself," that exists independent of our experience of it. In the philosophy of Kant, the noumenal world is the world of ultimate reality, as opposed to the world of the phenomenon, the world as it is experienced by human consciousness.

Ontology

The branch of philosophy concerned with the nature of existence and being.

Phenomenon

(*see* Noumenon)

Pragmatism
The view that truth is valid explanation—in other words, that a statement can be considered true if it describes a situation accurately enough to be useful.

Rationalism
The view that we acquire our knowledge of the world through reason rather than experience.

Relativism
The view in ethics that the morality of an action is dependent upon its context— for example, that different cultures and traditions have different views of what is right or wrong.

Skepticism
The view that it is not possible to have certain knowledge of anything.

Synthetic statement
(*see* Analytic statement)

Universe
(*see* World)

Utilitarianism
In ethics and political philosophy, the view that the morality of an action should be judged by its consequences, which should bring about the greatest good for the greatest number.

Validity
In logic, an argument is said to be valid if its conclusion follows from its premises. In a valid argument, the conclusion will be true if the premises are true, but if any of the premises are false, the conclusion may not be true.

World
In philosophy, "the world" (and sometimes "the cosmos" or "the universe") is used to mean everything that exists that we can have experience of, everything in empirical reality.

Index

Quercus

New York • London

ISBN 978-1-62365-337-8

Library of Congress Control Number:
2013913490

Distributed in the United States and Canada by
Random House Publisher Services
c/o Random House, 1745 Broadway
New York, NY 10019

Manufactured in China

10 9 8 7 6 5 4 3 2 1

www.quercus.com